THEN A
GENERAL EDITOR
MARJORIE REEVES M.A. PH.D.

The French Revolution

MIRIAM ROSENTHAL M.A.

Illustrated from contemporary sources

LONGMAN

LONGMAN GROUP LIMITED
*Longman House, Burnt Mill, Harlow, Essex CM20 2JE, England
and Associated Companies throughout the World.*

First published 1965
Twelfth impression 1983

ISBN 0 582 20403 8

ACKNOWLEDGEMENTS

We are grateful to the following for permission to reproduce copyright material:
Basil Blackwell & Mott Ltd. for material from *French Revolution Documents*, *The French Revolution* and *Leaders of the French Revolution* by J. M. Thompson; The Clarendon Press for material from *Orators of the French Revolution* by J. M. Stephens; The English Universities Press Ltd. for material from *Robespierre and the French Revolution* by J. M. Thompson; Hutchinson & Co. Ltd. for material from *The French Revolution* by A. Goodwin; Princeton University Press for material from *Twelve Who Ruled* by R. R. Palmer, and Routledge & Kegan Paul Ltd. for material from *A Social History of the French Revolution* by N. Hampson.
We have been unable to trace the copyright owner in *La Révolution Francaise* by A. Dayot and would welcome any information that would enable us to do so.
The map on page 61 is redrawn from *The French Revolution* by Thompson by permission of Blackwell Scientific Publications Ltd., and that on page 65 from *The French Revolution, A History by Thomas Carlyle*, edited by Ball and by courtesy of Cambridge University Press. For permission to reproduce photographs we are grateful to the following:
Bibliothèque Nationale—pages 48, 68, 75 and 98; Bulloz—pages 64, 69, 85 and 96; Landesbildstelle Wien-Burgenland—page 3 top; The Mansell Collection—page 99; Musée de Lille and Studio Gérondal—page 26; Musée Royaux des Beaux - Arts and A.C.L.—page 82; Ny Carlsberg Glyptotek—page 33; Paul Popper—page vi; Réunion des Musées Nationaux—pages 2, 4, 5, 7, 73, 86 and 90; Walden—page 3 lower, and the Trustees of the Wallace Collection—page 15 lower. All the others are by permission of the Trustees of the British Museum.

*Printed in Hong Kong by
Yu Luen Offset Printing Factory Ltd*

CONTENTS

TO THE READER

If you have ever seen a demolition gang beginning to tear down a beautiful house, you probably wondered why this was happening. The house looked perfectly all right. If you asked why the house was coming down, the answer would probably be that there was dry rot in it, but that a new one was going to go up on the same site. So these men were destroying something but only in order to put up something safer and stronger in its place which would please the owner better than the old house.

In a way this is what the French Revolution did for France. France is a country and not a house, but like a house it has people living in it. Just as there was something very wrong with this house, so was there something very wrong in France, as you shall see. The French Revolution tore down and then tried to build a safer, a better and a more modern France. Just as demolition is an ugly and sad thing to watch, so in many ways was it sad to watch the damage done as the Revolution did its work, but in the end, the Revolution did build a more up-to-date France.

You will read some of the speeches and part of the diaries which English and French people wrote during this Revolution. You will see pictures which Frenchmen drew or painted during or just after the Revolution.

One of the great things about the Revolution was that everyone took part in it. It was not just the work of a king and his ministers, but everyone living in France had a chance to make the France that the people wanted.

WHERE DID THE GREAT EVENTS OF THE REVOLUTION TAKE PLACE?

You will read about Versailles. This was the palace of the kings of France about fourteen miles from Paris.

You will read about many places in Paris. These are marked on the map on page 65. The letters after the names in this list will help you to find these places on the map:

BASTILLE (B)

This was a fortress given eight great towers in the fourteenth century; it was used mainly as a prison and for storing weapons.

CHAMP DE MARS (M)

Laid out as a parade ground, it was used for the great festivals of the Revolution.

CONCIERGERIE (CO)

The prison near the Palace of Justice.

CORDELIERS CLUB (C)

Political club which met in a former Franciscan friary.

FEUILLANT CLUB (F)

Political club which met in a former Benedictine monastery near the Tuileries.

INVALIDES (I)

Built by Louis XIV as a home for disabled soldiers, it was used to store weapons.

JACOBIN CLUB (J)

Political club which met in a former Dominican friary.

LYCEE LOUIS-LE-GRAND (L)

This was where Robespierre and Camille Desmoulins went to school.

PALAIS ROYAL (P)	The palace of the royal family of the dukes of Orleans. One of them had needed money, so he built shops and cafés in the gardens, and both the palace and these gardens became very important meeting-places during the Revolution.
PLACE DE LA RÉVOLUTION (G)	The square where executions by the guillotine took place.
TOWN HALL (TO)	The Hôtel de Ville, the home of the Paris town council.
TUILERIES (T)	The royal palace built in the 16th century; the home of Louis XVI and the royal family from October 1789 until the attack by Parisians on 10 August. The various National Assemblies and the Committee of Public Safety met here and in the Riding School (Manège).

Versailles—the palace seen from the park

I France and the French People

'Long live the King and Queen!' shouted the crowds outside the beautiful cathedral of Rheims where Joan of Arc had crowned Charles VII. They were shouting for the new king and queen of France, Louis Capet of the house of Bourbon, now Louis XVI, and Marie Antoinette of the house of Habsburg of Lorraine and Austria. Throughout France the bells pealed and the people rejoiced.

'Long live the nation, the tyrant is dead!' shouted the crowds standing in the Place de la Révolution in Paris, as the executioner held up the *guillotined* head of Louis XVI for them to see. Eighteen years had come between the shouts after the coronation in 1775 and the shouts after the death of Louis in 1793. The most powerful man in the land had died because his people had wanted him to die.

What a change! And there was another change. When Marie Antoinette and Louis had come to Paris after riding through the rich vineyards of Champagne, they visited the boys' school of Louis-le-Grand in the Rue St Jacques. There the boys and their teachers, who were Jesuit priests, were waiting to greet them. The greatest honour was to deliver a speech of welcome in Latin. The teachers chose the boy who was best at Latin. He was the seventeen-year-old Maximilien Robespierre, an orphan from Arras. Eighteen years later, in 1793, he came face to face with Louis and Marie Antoinette once again, but this time addressed to them the words of a bitter enemy.

Why were things so changed? The answer is that the Revolution had come.

What were the King and Queen like? The portrait of Louis you can see on the next page makes you think that he is very gentle and mild, and this he proved to be—in fact, he turned out to be also weak. He was not interested in being a strong king and preferred to let his ministers and powerful *courtiers* make decisions, while he went hunting, or spent time on his hobby which was making locks.

Many people thought that Marie Antoinette was the most beautiful woman at the court of Versailles. She was the daughter of the empress Maria Theresa of Austria. Her home had been in

Louis XVI

a court which in many ways was very different from the French court at Versailles near Paris. If you ever visit this and then go to Marie Antoinette's home in the Schönbrunn palace near Vienna you will still be able to feel this difference. They are both

Schönbrunn—The palace and the gardens

Schönbrunn—The Rose Room

magnificent, but the Schönbrunn is more friendly and less stiff. Maria Theresa had created within the palace a home for herself and her children. She enjoyed acquiring animals for her zoo, and placed near the animals' cages was a little house where the royal family used to have breakfast.

In this picture you see Marie Antoinette with her children.

Marie Antoinette and her children

Louis XIV had built Versailles to dazzle his subjects and the rest of Europe and his successors had continued to live in this grand and magnificent way. You can see Versailles in these pictures.

The Bull's Eye Window Drawing Room

Louis XVI's Library

Courtiers in the Gardens of Versailles

When Marie Antoinette arrived at Versailles she was supposed to learn how to behave in the stiff and serious manner of the French court. But she was a very lighthearted person and never managed to do this. She chose her own friends and they were not usually the most important people. Instead of spending days in the big palace itself which she found too grand and solemn, she preferred to stay in the tiny little palace called the Petit Trianon. She made the gardeners replan the gardens as she wanted them. A whole farm and country village were built for her, which you can see in the next picture. Peasants came to look after the farm, and there was a dairy where Marie Antoinette made butter. She liked to play at being a farmer's wife, but to most people living in France farming could never be a game. For them it meant long days of hard work in order to get enough to eat. Marie Antoinette would not starve if she had no milk to make butter from, but many farmers' wives did. By living as she pleased she made enemies at court and throughout France.

Marie Antoinette's House and Farm

At this time, that is, the eighteenth century, France was still very clearly divided into three '*estates*' or classes of people.

The first estate was that of the clergy or churchmen. The Church in France was extremely powerful because it owned vast lands which brought in much wealth. Many of the bishops and *cardinals* became important in the government of France. The Church also had great power because most of the teachers in schools and colleges were priests and also the tutors for the royal and noble families. The Church also controlled the hospitals and looked after the poor and aged. Although many of the priests at the top were powerful and wealthy, not all of them were; many country parish priests had no more money than the poor peasants and also had to work in the fields.

The second estate was that of the nobles. There were three different kinds. There were those who belonged to ancient royal and noble families; for example, the family of Orleans. They were called the nobles of the sword because originally they were the only men allowed to wear a sword. There were the nobles

7

who had been given noble titles because of the jobs they did, for example some of the judges. They were called the nobles of the gown to show that their title came from a particular office they held for which they wore a special gown. Lastly, there were the nobles who had bought their titles.

Not all the nobles were very great or wealthy like the men in the next pictures. Arthur Young, an Englishman who travelled in France just before the Revolution, describes in his diary how he met some nobles in Provence who were 'so poor that they plough their own fields'. However, he also describes lands which have been neglected and deserted because the noble owner preferred to be a 'glittering being' at the court at Versailles. Many nobles much preferred the life at Versailles to their country estates. At Versailles, they would spend their days in dressing in fine clothes or hunting. The pictures on the next pages give you some idea of their lives. The artist drew these pictures in the 1770s and 1780s and a writer added comments. In the first picture we see the following scene:

The young Duke of Sonfrac has just got out of bed. He is a fine looking young lord, extremely conceited and exceedingly impudent. He is already rich and is heir to a fortune which would make a hundred families wealthy. His *valet* is putting his stockings on for him; his butler is bringing a cup of chocolate, while his secretary—a *dapper* young priest destined one day to be the tutor of the young duke's son (if he has one), writes tender little notes to the many young women the bored duke is courting. He writes these partly out of his own head and partly takes down what the duke is saying. Suddenly a pretty perfume-seller with a turned-up nose comes in carrying a box with perfumes and gloves for the duke to buy.

In the next picture we see him almost ready. On the next page we see a family outing: the duke and duchess with their two children, the duchess's mother and the dog are about to go for a walk in the lovely forest of Marly near Versailles.

The last pictures show a concert and the magnificent evening dresses worn for an outing to the opera.

*The Young Nobleman
getting up in the
morning*

*The Rich Nobleman
almost ready to go out*

9

*An outing
to Marly*

A Concert in a Nobleman's House

Leaving the opera house

The third estate consisted of the 'professional' class, that is the lawyers and doctors and *administrators*, the merchants and shopkeepers, the factory workers, the servants, the shopworkers and the peasants. This estate was by far the largest. There were about half a million clergy and nobility. There were about twenty-five million people belonging to the third estate and of this number, the craftsmen, labourers, those employed in workshops, and peasants and servants, accounted for about twenty-four million.

Each estate had, in theory, certain duties to perform. The clergy educated, administered and nursed the people of France. The nobles provided many of the ministers and high government officials, the judges and the officers in the army and navy. The third estate provided the industries and food and the soldiers without which France could not survive.

The clergy and nobles had many *privileges*. Perhaps the most important was that they did not have to pay heavy taxes which made life a misery. All governments need money in order to keep the country safe and powerful. This money usually has to come from various taxes and in France one of the main ones was the *taille*. This was a very old tax first paid by those people who did not want to do military service in the army, but it was now paid by everyone except the nobles and clergy. Other taxes were like our purchase tax; that is, a certain amount of money was added to the price of goods, for example leather goods, and this extra money went to the government. There was a tax on salt called the *gabelle*. There were customs duties and as customs barriers stood not only at the frontiers between countries as they do today but also between towns, for example at the various entrances to Paris, a lot of money was taken by the government. The fair way with taxes is, of course, to share them round so that the rich pay more than the poor, but in France at this time, it was the nobles and clergy who were exempted from paying the heavy *taille*, while the peasants paid.

The Church did not pay taxes but was allowed to give presents of money to the government, and, of course, these gifts were too small. Out of an income of 120 million *livres*, the Church paid only two or three.

Since both the clergy and nobles were great landowners, they were also landlords over many peasants. Not only did they get high rents from their tenants, but also had the right to ask for additional gifts of farm produce and money. They could also order peasants to work for them in their fields and mills. The peasants built the roads and bridges and were forced into doing this. The nobles could hunt all over their estates and let game wander everywhere even if this meant that they ruined the tenants' land and crops. If a tenant killed a wild boar because it was ruining his land, the lord would send him to be a galley slave.

The nobles of the robe had power through their position as judges in the *parlements*. These were the highest courts of justice. If someone wished to try to obtain a different decision about his case he could appeal to this court for a final verdict. The *parlements*, especially the *parlement* of Paris, also had great influence over the laws of France. This was because the judges there had to register the orders made by the King and his council of ministers. Until the judges did this these orders were not laws and so no one need obey them. Therefore, if the judges did not like an order they could refuse to register it until the King and his ministers had changed it to please them. However, the King, by holding a special meeting which was called by the curious name of 'lit de justice', which means 'bed of justice', could ignore the parlement and force an order

Men's clothes in 1787

through. If he did this too often the judges got very angry and only a really strong King could afford to annoy them. Louis XVI was not strong enough.

The third estate had none of these privileges. Those who formed what we call the middle classes were often rich and the taxes did not harm them much, but they had no power in the country. They wanted to be able to take part in the government of France, but only the nobles and clergy could do this. In the next pictures and that on the previous page, you can see something of the life of the rich middle class.

Lady and lady's maid

*A game of
whist*

*A Visit (showing another well-to-do home in which the wealthier members of the third estate
might live)*

15

The rest of the third estate, those whom we would call the working classes, as well as having no privileges, were usually terribly poor. They earned very little and taxes and the high price of food were a dreadful burden.

Between 1715 and 1789 when the Revolution broke out, the money obtained from the hated gabelle, the salt tax, rose from twenty-three to fifty million livres. The livre was worth about a shilling of our money, so you can work out how much this was. To us it seems strange that salt could ever be such an extremely expensive item on a shopping list. In eighteenth-century France it was not only expensive but also an absolute necessity, for salt did what 'fridges' do now: it stopped food from going bad. The amount of the salt tax varied from town to town and therefore families tried to smuggle salt from towns where the tax was lower. If they were caught doing this, soldiers arrested them and a court sentenced them to the awful life of a galley slave. Even children got this punishment.

Not all peasants in France were very poor. There were peasant landowning families who were quite well off. These peasants still had to pay rent to the lords of the manor and also had to work on the lords' estates. There were other peasants called share-croppers. These peasants got half the seed and cattle from the lord and supplied their own tools and labour and then paid the taxes on the whole produce to the government, but had to give half of the produce to the lord. The poorest peasants worked for wages, like our farm labourers and came off very badly for they could not always find work, especially if the harvest was bad. They had no trade union and wages were often near starvation level. All the peasants suffered, too, because the noble landowners were always trying to get more money from them by discovering some ancient laws which said that they could ask for extra money.

The peasants also had to give money and farm produce to the clergy. In these pictures you can see the poor peasants faced

"Please God, deliver us from the customs barriers"

"Please God, deliver us from hunting rights"

"Please God, deliver us from military service"

"Please God, deliver us from the tax collectors"

17

with the various burdens. The customs barriers, the hunting rights of the landlords, having to go into the army, being dependent on wicked officials to whom they had to bring gifts—these were the burdens the peasants hated most.

Arthur Young describes how the peasants in France lived. In Payrac he saw women and children and ploughmen working in the stony fields without shoes or stockings. This would be because the tax on leather was so high that these families could not afford to buy shoes. At Islettes he met a woman who told him that 'the *taille* and the lord's rights are crushing us. We have one horse, one cow and a little land, we have to give 47 lb. of wheat and three chickens to the lord'. Because the peasants had to work so hard for the lords they often had no time for their own land. This poverty Arthur Young found everywhere he went. At Montauban, in Britanny, he wrote:

> The poor people seem poor indeed; the children terribly ragged, if possible worse clad than if with no clothes at all; as to shoes and stockings they are luxuries. A beautiful girl of six or seven years playing with a stick, and smiling under such a bundle of rags as made my heart ache to see her: they did not beg, and when I gave them anything, seemed more surprised than obliged.

Beggars

18

Making roads

Making wheels

Knife grinders

The village cobbler

The workers in the cotton and silk factories and shops, the street sellers, the cobblers also got bad treatment and little money. Unlike the peasants they could not even grow their own food and therefore depended entirely on wages. They suffered very much when the price of bread went up for that was what they lived on.

The needs and wishes of all the people of France, the King and Queen, the clergy and nobles, the lawyers, the peasants and the other workers, changed the history of France and Europe for they made the Revolution of 1789.

2 Money and Bread

In order to have enough to eat and have a roof over your head to protect yourself, you need money. If you think of a country as being a very large family, you realise that it also must have food and protection and therefore also needs money. In 1786 Louis XVI and his ministers needed money very badly to keep France fed and protected.

Calonne, one of the ministers, suggested that there should be a new land tax. The important thing about this tax was that the nobles and the clergy would have to pay it as well as everyone else. You can imagine that they would hate this, because until then they had never had to pay any land tax. Calonne also said that there would have to be changes in the government of the provinces of France. These changes would make the collection of the money easier, but they would annoy both the nobles and clergy because they would take away some of their power in the local government.

Who was to decide whether to accept this plan? The answer is an *assembly* of notables. The notables were noblemen, clergy and important lawyers. Out of these 144 men chosen, less than thirty belonged to the third estate. The very people who had to decide whether to accept the new tax and less power were the people these changes would hurt most. So you can imagine what happened. They refused. They said that the *parlement* of Paris must say yes first.

The *parlement* of Paris met in July 1787, but the magistrates there did not want these reforms either. Louis and his ministers were really worried and forced the reform through by the lit de justice (bed of justice). This made the magistrates furious and they refused to take any notice, so Louis sent them away from Paris in disgrace.

The *parlement* returned only when the magistrates had

partly given in to some reform. The magistrates then attacked the King's power to send anyone to prison without any form of trial or excuse. Louis and his ministers were angry, too, so they forced through reforms which would mean that all the *parlements* would no longer be able to stop the King's orders from becoming law.

Not only were the magistrates in Paris angry, but in Brittany and Dauphiné revolts broke out against the King.

Nobody was getting what he wanted—the nobles and clergy were not getting their powers back and the King and his

France in 1789

ministers were not getting money. Then Louis announced what everyone wanted to hear:

We need an assembly of our faithful subjects to help us to get over all the difficulties in which we find ourselves with regard to our *finances*. . . . We have decided to call an assembly of the estates of all the provinces, not only so that they may give their advice on everything we shall ask them to discuss, but also so that they may tell us the wishes and *grievances* of our people so that every kind of *abuse* will be reformed.

For the first time for 175 years the *Estates General* was to meet. Everyone wanted this for this would be the chance to get grievances removed. The estates were to meet at the palace of Versailles in May of the following year, 1789. In the ten months that followed not only did the people of France elect the people who were to speak for them, but they also made sure that they put their grievances down on paper in the form of 'lists of grievances'. The third estate insisted that no money was to go to the government without the consent of the people of France, because, after all it was the people who paid the taxes. Above all the people wanted a *Declaration* of the Rights of Man to become law.

The Declaration of the Rights of Man was the most important wish. It is what we ourselves feel is terribly important, although we usually take it for granted as we have these rights of *liberty* and *equality*. The third estate of Paris wrote: 'In every *political society* all men have equal rights.' This means that everyone in a country which has a government should be as free and equal as his neighbour. The man who is without a penny, without a job, has the right to do the same things as the rich prince, because he is equal to the prince. From this various rights follow which you shall read about. Because all men are born free it is wrong for some of them to be little better than slaves and have to build roads for their landlords. Also, everybody must share in governing the country, because everyone lives and works for the country. These were some of the ideas which people of the middle and working classes of France in

1789 were thinking about as they waited for the assembly of the Estates General. They wanted to change the picture you see below of the poor old man, who is the third estate, having to carry the fat and wealthy nobleman and clergyman. The old man is saying, 'We must hope that this will end some day.'

Rousseau, a man who wrote about how countries should be governed, had written a famous book called *The Social Contract*. In this he had talked about liberty or freedom and equality and how everybody should share in the government of the country, because it is not the king who has the most power, but the people. This book impressed many people. Those who had read the book explained its ideas to those who could not read it for themselves. All over France, not only the third estate, but even some of the clergy and nobles felt that the only right thing was for all the French people to share in the government and the wealth of France.

Everyone went on talking about the meeting of the Estates General, but in the middle of the excitement the corn harvest of 1788 failed. Now the peasants and workers could talk only of this, for they knew what would happen. Bread, the one thing which kept them alive, would get even more expensive. We forget how important bread is, but to people who cannot afford to buy meat and vegetables and eggs it is vital. For poor workers in France the year 1789 looked like being a grim and hungry one, but perhaps, they thought hopefully, the Estates General would save them from starvation.

Would the wealthy clergy and privileged nobles give up some money and power in order to make life fairer and bring more bread and happiness to the French and more strength to France? This was the great question in the minds of the French.

3 The Have-nots against the Haves

Opening of the Estates General

In this picture you can see the great hall at Versailles where the Estates General met on 4 May 1789, and you can see how splendid it was. The *deputies*—as the representatives for each estate were called—wore special costumes. The clergy wore crimson, scarlet, black, white and grey robes; the nobles wore black and cloth of gold.

The third-estate members were mostly lawyers in their early thirties. The third-estate members represented the unprivileged, the have-nots and fought against the privileged, those who had so much. One of them was Maximilien Robespierre, that schoolboy who had been chosen to make the Latin speech to Louis XVI in 1775. Robespierre was born in Arras in the north-east of France on 6 May 1758; you can work out how old he was when the Estates General met. His mother had died when he was thirteen and his father had left home, leaving

25

Maximilien to look after a younger brother, Augustin, and a sister, Charlotte. Maximilien won a scholarship to the school of Louis-le-Grand in Paris, where you first came across him. Fortunately there were aunts to look after the younger children, so he was able to go. Having done brilliantly at school, he studied to be a lawyer and then returned to work in Arras.

Robespierre

He was very hardworking. He was very neat, as this portrait shows. He does not look particularly striking but he does look wide-awake and sharp. He takes no notice of his dog 'Brount' but looks straight at us, as if he is about to speak to us.

Robespierre was very shy and rather an unloving person, without close friends. Instead of people, he seemed to love most the fight for freedom and equality. Of course, he wanted to win the freedom and equality for the people of France, but he did not care very much for the people themselves. He made no effort to talk to the poor and get to know them, but he fought for them. One of the splendid things about Robespierre was that he was ready to give away something he needed if he felt this was the right thing to do. He gave up a good job because it meant sentencing people to death, and he believed that no one should allow someone else to die. Because Robespierre was able to give things up, he expected others to be able to do this as well. In one of his first speeches at the Estates General as deputy for Arras, he cried out 'Let the bishops *renounce* a luxury which is an offence to Christian humility. Let them sell their coaches and horses, and give to the poor.' He was going to fight for the poor and the unprivileged, for equality which would make life fairer for them. He was prepared to fight to his death, to give away everything, but in the end, as you will see, he sacrificed other people's lives to try to achieve this.

Surprisingly, another important member of the third estate was a priest. This was the Abbé Sieyès who had chosen to represent the third estate rather than the clergy. He was born on 3 May 1748, at Fréjus in the south of France, and was ten years older than Robespierre. He had wanted to become a soldier or a mining engineer but at fourteen his family forced him to train to be a priest. But you can tell that he did not get on well with the clergy because he was not chosen to represent them. He was very learned and clever and serious. He worried very much about the miserable way the poor people of France lived. He realised that as long as the nobles and clergy continued to have so many privileges and powers, poverty would live on.

Sieyès was so depressed by the thought that France would

never improve that he saved up enough money to emigrate to America, where he thought there would be no poor people, but then the great opportunity came. The Estates General was to meet. Sieyès felt that at last there might be a chance of helping the poor. In January 1789 he published a short book called *What is the Third Estate?* In this he explained that the third estate was everything; the third estate was France. Yet though this was so, and the third estate did the work which kept France alive, it counted for nothing. Who governed France? Not the third estate, but lazy, useless nobles and clergy. The third estate must get a chance to govern and to speak the wishes of the people and obtain a *constitution* which will end unfairness. Sieyès had written down the ideas that were in the minds of so many people and he was ready to see that these ideas did not stay in a book, but that they became laws.

Another surprising representative of the third estate was a nobleman—Honoré Gabriel Riqueti, the Count of Mirabeau! But Mirabeau did not think like a nobleman; his ideas belonged instead to the third estate. Unlike either Robespierre or Sieyès, he had already become famous before the Revolution because of his wickedness. He was born at Bignon near Nemours on 9 March 1749, and, according to stories he was extraordinary even as a baby, for he was said to have two teeth already when he was born. Like most noblemen he went into the army and a marriage was arranged for him with a wealthy heiress whom he did not love. He fell in love with a married woman and ran away with her. A court sentenced him to death for this crime, but he was able to go to prison instead. Disgusted by prison conditions he wrote a great attack on the French prisons and wanted to reform them.

Mirabeau was a great talker and very charming and full of energy. Many people thought that because his way of life was evil, there was nothing good in him, but he fought against the bad conditions of the poor. He cheated, and to make money he published top secret documents which should never have come before the public, yet he managed to get elected to the Estates General for both Aix-en-Provence and Marseilles and chose to sit for Aix. Arthur Young describes how 'In every company, of every rank, you hear of the Count of Mirabeau's talents; that he is one of the finest pens in France, and the first *orator*.' You will, see how he rose to defend the liberty of the people against the privileged, and how he tried to prevent hurt to anyone, including the King and Queen.

At the first meeting of the Estates General people could see at once that the King and his ministers were not ready to make great reforms. They could see, too, that the nobles and clergy were not willing to give away money and power and unite with the third estate.

The first job which each estate had to do was to see that the deputies had been properly elected. The third estate wanted the three estates to meet together to do this, so that from the beginning they would each have an equal contribution to make. The nobles and clergy refused. For weeks they went on refusing. Their refusal is very important, because it showed that they would not give in to any wish of the third estate. They were very likely to refuse what the third estate also wanted, that is for each deputy to have a separate vote, instead of the clergy together having one vote, and the nobles together having one vote, and the third estate together having one vote. If each estate had one vote, then the third estate would always lose because the clergy and nobles would vote together against the third estate and it would therefore always be a case of two against one. If each deputy had a vote, the third estate would win—there were 600 third-estate deputies and they could count on the support of about 125 of the 300 clergy and about fifty out of the 300 nobles. You can now do a sum and find out what *majority* the third estate would get by this method of voting.

The third estate remained in the great hall alone. The

deputies refused to give the taxes which the King had asked for. They must have got very bored waiting, but they were stubborn. On 17 June they took action. They declared that THEY were the National Assembly—by themselves, without nobles or clergy. This was a revolutionary thing to do. Sieyès and Mirabeau had influenced them. They declared that:

National Assembly is the only title appropriate to the assembly as things are because the members have come at the wishes of practically the whole nation; there can only be one single body of representatives, and no deputy, in whatever order or class, has any right to work apart from the present assembly, even if nobles or clergymen have elected him.

This was a great attack on Louis and on the nobles and clergy. For the deputies of the third estate were saying that the only people who mattered and who ought to have the last word were they themselves, and that without them the King, the nobles, the clergy were nothing. They also said that if the King and ministers tried to destroy the National Assembly, then no one in France would have to pay taxes, because no National Assembly meant that the people had no representatives to agree to the taxes.

Marie Antoinette and other members of the royal family and court persuaded Louis to order guards to close the meeting hall of the third estate. On 20 June, in the pouring rain, the third-estate deputies walked to their hall. They found soldiers everywhere and, of course, could not get in. They would not give in, however, and went into the tennis court instead (in France at this time, tennis was played in a walled and roofed court with a gallery for visitors. It was called royal tennis although you did not have to be royal to play it). Here the deputies swore an oath to keep together until France had a fair constitution:

Nothing can prevent [the Assembly] from continuing its discussions wherever it may be forced to meet; all members of this Assembly shall here and now take a solemn oath never to abandon the Assembly and to go on meeting wherever it has to until the constitution of the realm is set up.

30

In other words, no one, not even the King, the greatest power in the land, was going to order them about. They spoke for the people and would do only what the people wanted.

The Tennis Court Oath

In this picture you can see the scene in the tennis court. The most famous artist of the Revolution, Jacques Louis David, drew this. You can see all the excitement that the deputies felt. They waved their hats in the air, hugged each other and shouted. The man standing on the table is Bailly, later to become mayor of Paris; he is making the deputies take the oath. Sitting at the table at the right of Bailly is Sieyès. The man standing by the chair with his head pushed back and clasping his chest with both hands is Robespierre. In front on the right, with legs apart and with his left arm outstretched holding his hat, while raising his right hand for the oath is

Mirabeau. Visitors are staring in through the gallery. On the left through the window, although you can hardly see it, a thunderbolt is striking the Palace of Versailles which to the poor stands for everything they hate and find most unfair.

Meanwhile in Paris and the rest of France everyone was waiting and talking excitedly or reading the latest pamphlets which came out every day. Those who could not read listened to those who could:

> The coffee houses in the Palais Royal are not only crowded within, but other expectant crowds are at the doors and listening open mouthed to certain orators who from chairs or tables *harangue* each his little audience: the eagerness with which they are heard and the thunder of applause they receive for every *sentiment* of more than common *hardiness* or violence against the present government cannot easily be imagined.

This is how Arthur Young described Paris. He also described a visit to the National Assembly, where, he said, the meeting was terribly noisy. A hundred deputies would get up and shout at the same time, while the audience in the galleries clapped their hands when they approved of a speech.

What did Louis feel about this? On 23 June he spoke to all the deputies of the three estates. He was not going to give the freedom that the National Assembly wanted.

One of the King's servants ordered the estates to leave and the nobles and clergy meekly followed the King out of the great hall. But the National Assembly refused to go. The King sent the Marquis de Brézé to tell them to go away. Bailly said they would not go and then Mirabeau spoke to de Brézé. In the picture opposite you can see that everyone stood up with him. This is what Mirabeau said:

> Sir, you are a stranger in this assembly, you have no right to speak here; return to those who have sent you and say to them that we shall not stir from our places save at the point of the bayonet.

You can see the amazed expression on the face of de Brézé and feel that the deputies are ready to follow Mirabeau.

Mirabeau and the Marquis de Brézé

Once again the third estate deputies had shown that no one could order them about. Louis then pretended to give in to the third estate, by ordering the clergy and nobles who had not yet joined the National Assembly to do so at once. However, Louis also took the advice of his ministers and secretly prepared to threaten the National Assembly with an attack by soldiers. Who would save the Assembly?

4 Paris Fights for Freedom

July 1789 was hot and the people of Paris were frightened—frightened that Louis XVI would order soldiers to attack them in their fight for freedom, for Versailles was only about fourteen miles from Paris. In spite of their fear the Parisians were ready to fight back.

Indeed, they did not wait to see what the King would do. They rushed to the customs barriers and burned or tore them down. They hated them because here they had to pay customs money on the food coming into Paris and this made food too expensive to buy.

On 12 July Louis dismissed the popular minister, Necker, whom the people felt was their friend. There was excitement and anger. In this picture you can see the Parisians crowding round the young Camille Desmoulins in the Palais Royal.

Camille Desmoulins in the gardens of the Palais Royal

Camille was a fighter for the freedom of the people. He had been to the same school as Robespierre and became famous as a *journalist*. Here you see him with a gun in his hand, standing on the table shouting to the Parisians to show their anger at the dismissal of Necker and to fight for their own freedom. He tore a leaf off the tree next to him and pinned it to his coat as a badge of freedom and told all those who supported freedom to do the same. So you can imagine that, as the excited crowd, with the men waving their sticks in the air, snatched the leaves, the trees were soon bare.

Still afraid of Louis's soldiers, the Parisians rushed to find guns and gunpowder. On the morning of Tuesday, 14 July, they ran through the great courtyards to the Invalides and took away the cannons. Then they took guns and rushed to the great fortress of the Bastille. The Bastille had eight enormous towers, terribly thick walls and a wide moat. It was used as a prison and the people of France hated it because of this. It was also used to store guns and weapons. Now the Parisians wanted these guns to defend themselves. Standing outside the moat, they asked the governor of the Bastille if they could have guns. He said that he would give them to them and that he would not shoot at the crowd unless they tried to get into the fortress. A few minutes later two men had managed to get in and let down the great drawbridge across the moat for the mob to swarm in. The governor therefore let one of his men shoot at the crowd and soon there was a real battle, as you can see in the picture on the next page. The Parisians captured this great fortress in only four hours and murdered the governor.

A nobleman told Louis what had happened and Louis said 'Is this a rebellion?' 'No Sire,' answered the nobleman, 'this is a revolution.' Louis finally realised this. The National Assembly had used words to try to change France; these had not been enough. Now Paris had used force and had shown that Paris, not the King, was the strongest power in the land. The

35

Storming of the Bastille

Fall of the Bastille was a great event. It is still celebrated in France today, and if you are ever in Paris on 14 July, you can drink and dance in the streets all night under the fairy lights and watch fireworks flash across the sky.

On 17 July men started to tear down the remains of the Bastille, so today all you can see are the stones which marked the spot where it stood. Also on the 17th, Louis came to Paris and accepted at the town hall the new flag of France. The new flag, the tricolour, is still the flag of France. It has red, blue and white stripes; the red and blue are the colours of Paris, the white was the colour of the Bourbon family to which Louis belonged. Robespierre was one of the members of the National Assembly who came with Louis to Paris. He describes this event as a scene which those who were there could never forget, for, in fact, they were seeing the King giving his crown to the people. The people were to be the rulers of France.

5 Fear and Freedom

In the rest of France the peasants were frightened and angry. They did not know what was going on in Paris, as there were hardly any newspapers, and when the papers did come, they were days late. The Great Fear was spreading through France.

Many peasants were sure that fierce bandits in the pay of Marie Antoinette and the nobles of the court at Versailles were riding through the countryside murdering and robbing every person they met. They also thought that these wild brigands would set fire to the precious corn, and if this happened there would be no bread. Arthur Young tells us that at a place called Colmar everyone was saying that Marie Antoinette had a plot to blow up the National Assembly with a mine and get the army to murder everyone in Paris.

The peasants were hungry as well as afraid. Last year's harvest had been so bad and this year's had not been brought in yet, so that there was little bread. The peasants had no money, yet they had to go on paying high rents to the nobles for whom they worked so hard. The fear and hunger were too much.

Throughout France peasants began to attack their lords. They went to the castles and threw flaming torches at the beautiful houses so that they could burn the papers which said that they had to pay these high rents and give part of their crops to the lords. Like the Parisians, they felt that they had to save themselves from Louis and Marie Antoinette and their court. They were also having their revenge, for the nobles had often treated them little better than slaves. They burned the castles and many nobles and their families were forced not only to leave their castles, but France as well. Arthur Young met a noble family at an inn in Burgundy who had escaped from the flames and had lost everything except the land on which the castle had stood, but to this they did not dare go back.

When the National Assembly heard of these attacks the members knew that they would have to act quickly if they wanted this burning and murder to stop. The nobles realised this too. On the night of 4 August, the nobles agreed to give up their special rights and privileges and so did the clergy. The hunting rights, the forced labour, the gifts of farm produce, all these were to end. The great differences between the first and second estates and the third estate were to go. The leaders of the Revolution wished to be fair to everyone, so the National Assembly said that there would be some *compensation* for the loss.

This was a great step forward towards the day when all people would be free and equal. In the picture below you can see the nobles and clergy talking about their decision and getting up to tell the president of the assembly that they agreed to it.

The French people were so happy when they heard what had happened. Not only had the hated hunting rights gone, but

The Nobles give up their privileges

for the first time every job would be open to every citizen, so the merchants and lawyers were happy because at last they might get jobs which for centuries only nobles had been able to have. One result of the new laws was that everyone went shooting. Arthur Young wrote:

> For a few days past, I have been pestered with all the mob of the country shooting; one would think that every rusty gun in Provence is at work, killing all sorts of birds. The National Assembly has declared that every man has a right to kill game on his own land.

Compare the cartoon on page 23 with the one below.

The old man says: "I knew we would get our turn one day"

Now the priest and nobleman carry the old man. The old man looks so much happier and younger. He is saying that 'I knew our turn would come one day.' On a stick over his shoulder hangs a rabbit which he has just shot—something he could never have done before 4 August.

The next great event in the Assembly was on 26 August. The members drew up the Declaration of the Rights of Man and the Citizen which everyone had cried out for. It said that 'Men are born free and with equal rights' and the reason why we live in a country is to protect the right to be free, the right to own things, the right to find what makes us happy and the right to fight back when someone attacks our freedom. We are free to do what we please as long as we do not hurt others, we can choose where we live and the job which we would like to do. This Declaration was terribly important; everyone who could read got hold of a copy to read for himself and for those who could not yet read. It was the guide for the French people in their fight for these rights. The French wanted freedom and equality and happiness not only for themselves but for the whole world. They wanted the negro slaves in the lands owned by France to be free; they wanted to bring freedom to all the peoples of the world who did not have it.

In many countries the coming of this Declaration caused great rejoicing. Revolutionary clubs began to meet. The people of Belgium and Holland and Germany, who had harsh rulers, were happy that the French were fighting against the harsh rule they had suffered for hundreds of years. At the same time the rulers of these countries trembled for they were afraid that they would be the next to lose their power if their people followed the example of the French.

What did Louis feel about this great document? We do not know; we only know that he followed the advice of the nobles at court. He refused to accept what the National Assembly had done. What would happen now?

6 The Women of Paris Fight for Bread

While the people of Paris were going hungry because there was no bread, Louis and the court entertained Flemish soldiers with great banquets at Versailles. These soldiers were ready to leave the tables piled high with meat and bread and fruit and wine and go and fight the starving Parisians to defend the royal family and court.

In Paris the men and women surrounded the bakers' shops. They queued for a tiny portion of bread. They queued all day and knew that perhaps tomorrow there would be none at all. Sometimes they queued the whole day and still got nothing. Lots of the workshops were empty because the workers had to go to queue for bread. If they did this of course they got no money and in the end had nothing to buy food with.

The people were getting so desperate that they rushed into the town hall to ask the mayor to do something for them. Many of the people there were women and they soon began to listen to a young man who got up to talk to them. His name was Stanislas Maillard and he told them that they could not just let things get so bad, they, the women, must do something. It was up to them to go to Versailles and bring back not only bread, but also the royal family. First they must go and fetch axes and pikes and guns, because Maillard knew that the women by themselves would not be frightening enough.

On 5 October the women marched to the Palace of Versailles. In the picture on the next page you can see them armed with the guns, axes and pikes they went to fetch. They ran into the palace and wanted to see Marie Antoinette. Marie Antoinette stood for everything they hated most about the unfair way in which princes and nobles had ruled France. Marie Antoinette never had to work, she did not have to carry heavy baskets on her head, or stand on her feet all day, or have to make a meal

41

The women of Paris march to Versailles

for a starving husband and eight or ten children out of dried beans and occasionally a few ounces of stringy meat. Marie Antoinette never had hands which were sore from scrubbing floors and clothes. She only played at working in her dairy. She did not know what the lives of these women were like. Now these women hissed and shouted at her and asked her for bread.

The popular Lafayette, a hero of the American War of Independence, persuaded the royal family to appear at a balcony and greet the swarming crowd below. It was brave of Marie Antoinette to appear, but it did no good. The crowd continued to scream.

There was only one thing to do. Louis, Marie Antoinette and their children, together with the court and the National Assembly, had to come to Paris. The royal family left Versailles never to return again. They came to Paris to face the people you can see in the picture opposite.

This was yet another victory for the Parisians. Although Louis had brought in soldiers from Flanders, the Parisians

The Royal Family arrives in Paris

had won; they had forced the royal family and the National Assembly to move to Paris to live under their watchful eyes.

The royal family came to live in the palace of the Tuileries. From 19 November the Assembly met in the old riding school of the palace. The job of the Assembly was to make a constitution for France. You will see what this meant to the people of France.

7 The New France

From November 1789 until August 1792 the deputies met in the Riding School. The hall was not very comfortable; it was far smaller than the room the deputies had used at Versailles. They sat in two blocks like our members of parliament in the House of Commons. Those on the right were usually supporters of the King and his ministers, while those on the left were usually against the King because they wanted great changes in France which he would not allow.

For many of the deputies it was their first chance of living in Paris. After their meetings were over they could walk in the gardens of the Palais Royal opposite, where the talk was of the events of the day or of the passers by. The gardens were the scenes of thefts, lovers' meetings, fashion parades and violent arguments. There were shops and there were cafés.

The deputies could also go to the political clubs. The most important were the Jacobin Club and the Cordeliers Club. Both clubs wanted great changes in France. They did not want the King to have power, because they believed that the people should be king and that they should have the power. Not all the club members were deputies. Lots of students, and shop and factory workers belonged to the Cordeliers Club because membership only cost a penny a month.

If you go to France today you will easily be able to find groups of men talking over a glass of wine or a cup of coffee. They love to talk about politics, the way France is governed, and what is wrong and how the wrong can be put right. You can imagine then that in 1790, when the people knew that a new government was going to come, the café tables were buzzing with conversation, with ideas on what changes would come to France.

The changes that did come were written down in the Constitution of 1791 and the deputies in the Assembly decided on them. You are going to hear about them all now, but in fact they took many months to come about.

The first part of the Constitution you already know about, because it was the Declaration of Rights. The rest of the Constitution tried to put these rights into practice, to see that justice was done and that men should have equal opportunities.

What happened to the King? The King lost a lot of power. He could no longer bring in laws, nor could he prevent the laws which the Assembly introduced from coming into force, even if he disliked them. This was very important. Instead of having to obey one man even when he did cruel and unjust things, the French people would now make laws for themselves, which was much more fair. They were going to make these laws in the National Assembly, but of course twenty-six million people could not leave their work and come to Paris, so they would choose people to represent them.

There was another change. The people were going to choose their representatives by voting for them as we do in England at a general election. However, the French deputies did not represent a class of people as they used to do, now they represented the French people. Nor did they, as our members of parliament do, represent a particular area, but Paris, for example, chose a deputy and this deputy did not represent Paris alone but the whole of France.

However, not all the French people were going to have the vote or be able to be deputies. Only those who paid a certain amount of taxes could vote or be a deputy. In other words, the very poor did not have a chance. Protestants, Jews, actors and domestic servants also did not have these rights. One member of the Assembly was very angry about this: Robespierre. He got up again and again to speak in favour of those left out. He said that it was against the rights of man to let some have the vote but not all, because all men are equal. Robespierre said:

Do you really think that a hard and laborious life produces more vices than luxury, ease, and ambition: have you really less confidence in the virtue of our labourers and artisans than in that of tax-collectors, courtiers, and the so-called nobility? . . . In the poor are found honest and upright souls and a good sense and energy that one would seek long and in vain among a class that looks down upon them.

Robespierre championed the poor against men who were snobbish enough to think that because men were poor this meant that they had no right to vote. He fought in vain, and the vote remained only with the better-off citizens. However, he did win one victory and got the vote for the Protestants, Jews and actors.

What else did this Constitution do? It said that the organisation of France was to be more sensible. Instead of lots of different kinds of local government, there was to be one kind throughout France. There were to be eighty-three Departments and these still exist today. Each Department had the same kind of government.

Another great change took place in the way judges were allowed to deal with crime and punishment and the problems which arose when people quarrelled over who owned land and property. One of the most unfair things about France before the Revolution was the cruel way in which many judges behaved and the terrible punishments they gave to those who broke the law. At the courts where the nobles had been judges many peasants had had a very hard time. The Revolution wanted fair treatment for everybody. The Constitution took away all the courts which had been unfair or too powerful, so the nobles' courts went and so did the proud *parlements*. The people were to elect the judges and the government was to pay them. Punishments were to be less cruel. Punishment was to help people, to teach them to do no more wrong. Robespierre fought for the ending of the punishment of death. He felt that it was better to let a hundred guilty men go free rather than let one innocent man die. He was afraid of sentencing a man to death in case some information came later and proved that the man had not committed the crime for which he had had to die. However, Robespierre could not persuade the Assembly to agree with him and the death penalty remained.

The Constitution reorganised the army so that for the first time men who were not of noble birth could become high-ranking officers.

There were to be no more noble titles; soon the great title was not Your Grace, or Your Highness, but Citizen.

So you see that the Constitution tried to bring freedom and equality.

8 Hard Times for the Clergy and the Nobles

In this picture you can see what was happening to some of the noble families in Paris. The Parisians have rushed in and started to throw the beautiful furniture through the closed windows! You can imagine that this was too much for the nobles

Porisians attack the house of the Duke of Castries

and many of them began to leave France, for to remain was too dangerous.

As you have read, the titles of Duke and Count now meant nothing. France had changed so much that now the important title was Citizen. Everyone was a citizen, whether he was rich or poor, born in a castle or a dingy house in the backstreets of a town.

Life also became different for the clergy. The government still needed a lot of money to save France. The Church, because of its lands, had a great deal of money, so the government decided to take these lands away. Instead the government paid the clergy a fixed wage. This was better for the poorer country clergy who had often nearly starved, but would now get a regular income, but you can see that for the wealthy it was a sad change. In the cartoon below you see how thin the clergyman has become after losing his wealth. Another difference

The thin priest remembers the good old days

was that all the clergy, even the bishops, were to get their jobs by election. In each Department and district voters would elect them. This was a much fairer system because until now many unsuitable people had become bishops only because they had powerful friends at court who put them into these jobs.

Although this new system may seem fairer to us, and was following the system used by the early Christians, to many of the clergy concerned it was very annoying. The trouble came when the government decided that, as the clergy were now servants of France, they should swear an oath to watch over the faithful believers entrusted to them and to be loyal to the nation, the law and the King, and to uphold the Constitution. Many of the clergy disliked the reforms and the Constitution, for example, those who were teachers, because their schools lost the money necessary to keep them going, which was, of course, not fair. Half the clergy refused to take the oath. Some waited to hear what the Pope, Pius VI, had to say. Because France was a Roman Catholic country, the clergy had to obey not only the laws of the land, but also the wishes of the head of the Church who is the Pope. Pius VI did not like the Revolution. He told the French clergy that they should not accept the new laws. So can you imagine what happened?

The French clergy had a great problem. Should they obey the laws of France and earn the hatred of the Pope, and in this way also, some felt, the hatred of God, or should they obey the Pope and earn the hatred of the French government and many of the people? They split into two groups over this question and in the end they almost split France in two, because some agreed with one group and some with the other. In a Breton village some villagers stoned the priest for taking the oath and when he changed his mind and said he did not want to keep his word other villagers came and stoned him.

Many of the parish priests and bishops and the monks and nuns did not like what was happening and left France. You

50

can see some of them huddled together sadly in this picture.
What happened to the monasteries, to the castles, to the

Monks and nuns forced to emigrate

acres of land that many nobles and clergy had left? Many of
the beautiful castles lay empty until they were little more than
ruins but the parks, where for so many years noble families
had walked and hunted and danced, were sold and put under
the plough. The plough soon came to the church lands as well.
Everyone who could bought the lands. Even some of the better-
off peasants were able to do this.

The power of the clergy and nobles inside France had really
gone. The first and second estates had lost the battle with the
third estate. The only way the nobles and clergy, who did not
like what had happened, could hope to win back what they
had lost was by getting help from foreign rulers.

Someone else felt this, too. This was Marie Antoinette, but
she had to persuade Louis to agree to her plan. For the time
being Louis would not listen. In July 1790 he took part in the
great celebration of the first anniversary of the fall of the
Bastille. For months preparations had gone on. Everyone in
Paris and throughout France helped—soldiers, workmen,

students and schoolboys, the young and the old. On 14 July, thousands of people came to the Champ de Mars in Paris. Twenty thousand came from the provinces to swear loyalty to the Constitution on the altar of the fatherland. They sang and fired gun salutes. After the serious part of the day there were firework displays and illuminations in the Champs Elysées and dancing all night in the streets.

Everything seemed to be going so well but the religious changes had made many unhappy. They now made Louis unhappy, so that he agreed to follow Marie Antoinette's plan. Marie Antoinette believed that no one in France was ready to help them. One man, however, tried to help, Mirabeau, who had been sending notes of advice and plans to help them, because he felt that for the good of France the King must have some power. Marie Antoinette took no notice of his advice as she disliked Mirabeau and preferred to follow her own advice. Marie Antoinette paints a sad picture of the life of the royal family:

> Our health is still good, but it would be better, if we could see a gleam of happiness in our surroundings. For ourselves there is no more hope of it, whatever happens. It is a king's duty, I know, to suffer for others; and, heaven knows, we are doing it to the full. Perhaps some day people will realise this.

9 Escape

Marie Antoinette was sure that there was only one thing to do. She wanted the royal family to leave France and force her brother Leopold, the powerful Emperor of Austria, to help them. They would have to escape secretly, because you can imagine that the French people would be angry if they found out what was happening.

This was the plan. Marie Antoinette and Louis were to travel in a coach borrowed from a Russian baroness. The governess of the royal children was to pretend to be the baroness with a forged passport. Louis and Marie Antoinette were to disguise themselves as the valet and governess of the royal children, also in disguise. At various points along the route to the eastern *frontier* of France (see the map on page 61), troops would be waiting to escort them to the next point. If anyone asked about the troops, the answer was to be that the coach contained treasure which needed an armed escort.

They had to get away. They knew that what they wanted to do would risk the safety of France and also the good things that the Revolution had brought, because, by leaving France and trying to raise an army abroad, they might bring civil war to France. That would be a war in which one Frenchman would fight another Frenchman in France, because not all Frenchmen approved of the Revolution and they would therefore help the royal family if there should be a war.

On the evening of Monday 20 June, the escape began. The royal family left the Tuileries by a secret exit. They had the longest day in the year ahead of them. It was very hot and they were very crowded inside the Russian baroness's coach. They rode a hundred miles to Chalons. So far all was well and soon they would have the armed escort, but then a disaster happened. The man in charge of the escort had expected the royal party at half-past two, he had waited until four o'clock and then went away and also told the next band of soldiers that the royal family were obviously not coming on this day.

The royal party had to travel on without an escort. They arrived at Ste Menehould, but once again there were no troops waiting. They changed horses and foolishly Louis and Marie Antoinette let themselves be seen. The *posting-master*, Drouet, recognised Louis from the portrait on the money with which he paid for the horses. So now the chase began.

Drouet and another man rode on horseback to Varennes. They got there long before the royal party because they took a path which a coach could not have managed. They arranged for the blocking of the bridge across which the royal coach would have to cross. Only a few yards away from the horses and soldiers who would have brought them across the frontier to safety, Louis and his family came face to face with a group of armed men. Escape was impossible.

Louis and Marie Antoinette and their children returned to Paris under armed guard. It must have been a terrifying journey. The journey to Varennes had been full of suspense, but at least they knew that if all went well there would be freedom and safety at the end. The journey back to Paris was very different. They did not know what was in store for them. For three and a half days they rode back, always passing through crowds of angry country and townspeople who had come out to see the royal family whom they now called *traitors*. Some of the people in the angry crowds had, long ago, cheered Marie Antoinette when she first came to France to marry Louis.

The royal family arrived in Paris. There was silence, for both applause and hissing were forbidden. The silence of thousands of people is, perhaps, even more terrifying than boos and hisses. What would happen to Louis and Marie Antoinette? Would Marie Antoinette's brother, Emperor Leopold, still come to the rescue?

10   France Wishes to be Free

When the members of the Assembly met in Paris to discuss the royal flight, they declared that they would see to it that France would be free because this is what France wanted. For the time being, therefore, Louis would have no power, but the Assembly hoped that it would not be so long before they could give him some power back.

To the Parisians in particular this punishment seemed far too mild. The King had been a traitor to them, it was for them to decide on his punishment. Although it is true that the Assembly represented the people of France and so had the right to say what should happen to the King, was the Assembly finding a suitable punishment? No, not in the opinion of the thousands who signed a *petition* which called for the *abdication* of Louis, because he had committed a crime against France.

The Cordeliers Club had encouraged the Parisians and on Sunday 17 July, they rushed to the Champ de Mars and filled almost twenty books with their signatures. Those who were either too young or too old to write got others to guide their hands so that they too could write their names. At about half past seven in the evening, members of the Parisian guard led by Lafayette, with guns and swords in their hands, came to get rid of these petitioners. There was a warning shot above their heads. Still the crowd remained, in any case it was difficult for so many people to leave the Champ de Mars quickly. The soldiers were impatient and so they shot at the crowd who were, of course, unarmed: about twelve people died and thirty or forty were wounded. This was an event which the Parisians never forgot and never forgave. For it was an attack on liberty, the liberty that the Revolution fought for—Lafayette, once their hero, and his men had attacked six thousand people for saying and writing what they thought.

For some of the leaders of the Revolution life in Paris became dangerous; Camille Desmoulins, for example, had to go into hiding. The Jacobin Club split into two groups and one group formed the Feuillant Club which met near the Tuileries. The Feuillants shared the ideas of Mirabeau who had died in April. They wanted to save the Revolution by bringing together again the King and the people of France, and they wanted the King to have more power.

Meanwhile the Assembly continued to meet. It had only a few more weeks to go before the French people elected a new one. Robespierre had persuaded the Assembly to say that none of the present members could stand for election to the next Assembly. He said that it would not be fair to the French people because these members had been meeting, either in Versailles or Paris, for two and a half years and so it would be fairer to have people who had been with the French people and knew what they wanted.

What was happening to Louis and Marie Antoinette? Marie Antoinette was very unhappy. She wrote to her brother Leopold:

> It is for the emperor to put an end to the disturbances of the French Revolution. Compromise has become impossible. Everything has been overturned by force and force alone can repair the damage.

In other words she wanted Leopold to come with a great army and destroy the Revolution. Leopold was not quite ready to do this but many feared that soon he would be.

Louis, who did not like to quarrel with anyone, agreed to sign the Constitution of 1791. At last there was something to rejoice over again. On Sunday 18 September, Paris celebrated. In the morning there were great gun salutes and no coach could move for the crowds of people. There was a balloon ascent in the Champs Elysées. There were fairylights everywhere.

The crowds shouted for Robespierre, 'Long live Liberty! Long live Robespierre! Long live the *Incorruptible*!' The crowds carried him through the streets in triumph. For all along he had fought for the people. A few weeks later he visited his home town of Arras and found the town lit up in his honour.

The Assembly finished and a new one took its place. The old members went home except for a few important ones like Robespierre. Because he could not make speeches in the Assembly he made them in the Jacobin Club. The club met in what had been a friary for Dominican friars or Jacobins as they were nicknamed in the Rue St Honoré. You can see a meeting in this picture. The club became very important. Soon

The Jacobin Club

both the members of the Assembly and the members of the Jacobin Club began to talk about a very great problem, the problem of war or peace.

11 War or Peace

On 1 October 1791 the new Assembly, called the *Legislative* Assembly, met for the first time in the Riding School at the Tuileries.

A Prussian visitor described their meetings and showed that they were full of excitement:

> The deputies carelessly dressed come and go, slapping their boots with their canes, coughing, spitting, speaking at the tops of their voices, and calling to one another across the hall. The President is constantly ringing his huge bell, and shouting, 'Take your seats, Gentlemen!' till he has no voice left. The ushers clap their hands in vain till they are tired out. The deputies pay no more attention than schoolboys who have got out of hand, and know that the old master will not strike them. An orator may be making a speech, hundreds of deputies go on talking just the same. Somebody may interrupt him, or make loud remarks: often the uproar becomes *intolerable*.

So this was how the 745 deputies behaved. They were talking and shouting about the fate of France. They spent nearly all the day in the Assembly. The meetings began at nine in the morning and went on until two or three in the afternoon. Then they started again at six in the evening and went on until nine.

Outstanding among the deputies was Jacques Pierre Brissot. He was a journalist who brought out a newspaper called *The Patriot*. In this he defended the Revolution. He devoted himself to the Revolution and put it before his family who had to live on very little. He was more of a writer than a talker, but he became a leader of a group of deputies about whom you shall hear more. One of them was the brilliant young lawyer Vergniaud. Another became a minister in the government. This was Roland who had a beautiful wife who was very interested in politics. Later on, because so many of the deputies who followed Brissot came from the area of southern France called the Gironde, they became known as the Girondins.

58

One of the first things the Assembly did was to make a law about the *émigrés*. These were French people who had left France and were now living in Germany or Austria and the Austrian empire. Nearly all of them were nobles or clergy. The Assembly felt they were dangerous because they were likely to try and get foreign help to attack France and the Revolution which they hated. The Assembly said that if the *émigrés* did not return to France by a certain date, then they would never be able to come back again and they would lose all the land and property they had in France.

In this picture you can see the sad state of a nobleman.

The nobleman says: "That which I was—
that which I am—
that which I shall be"

Once everything was wonderful, the peasants brought flowers to him and his family and they lived in their beautiful castle. Then they had to leave to save their lives. Now what is left? Nothing better than the life of a tramp and beggar on the road.

The deputies had to think of the French who were still in France and could not spare tears for those who had left. They had to decide a terrible question: should France make war on Austria and Prussia, countries with perhaps the strongest armies in Europe? For months they talked about this. Brissot and Vergniaud made fiery speeches to convince the deputies that France must go to war.

Brissot said that only through war could they get rid of the enemies who were doing their best to kill the Revolution. They were terrified of the enemies inside France and the *émigrés* who would get help from Emperor Leopold and the King of Prussia. Vergniaud told the deputies: 'Detest war; it is man's greatest·crime and most ghastly plague'. He also said in January 1792:

> Our Revolution has spread great alarm among all the Kings: it has set the example for the destruction of *despotism* which keeps them going. The *despots* hate our Constitution because it makes men free, and they wish to reign over slaves. You can see this hatred in the help and protection they are giving to the *émigrés*. To arms! To arms! Citizens, you are free men so defend your freedom, live up to the hopes mankind has for you, or else you will not deserve its pity when misfortune comes.

The Girondins also felt, as Robespierre suspected, that a war would keep them in power and make them the rulers of France. They wanted the enemies of the Revolution to be crushed abroad so that nothing would harm trade in France, especially the trade of the great seaports like Bordeaux. They wanted to prevent harm from coming to their followers, many of whom were great merchants who depended on the trade of these seaports.

Meanwhile, at the Jacobin Club, Robespierre told the members that a war was wrong. War would not protect liberty and equality and *fraternity*, that is, the good things of the Revolution. It would play into the hands of the despots, and the tyrants.

Robespierre at the Jacobin Club lost and Vergniaud and Brissot at the Assembly won. Only seven deputies voted against war.

On 20 April 1792, France declared war on Austria and Prussia 'to defend her liberty and independence'.

The French Revolutionary Wars 1792–1794 *and The Flight to Varennes* (*marked* . . . .)

If you look at this map you can see that many enemies surrounded France. In those days Belgium was not an independent country but part of the Austrian empire known as the Austrian Netherlands. It was here that the great battles of

61

1792 to 1794 took place. The French Revolutionary Wars, however, lasted much longer than two years; they went on for nearly twenty-five years. England, Sweden, Spain, the Italian states, Holland, Switzerland and almost the whole of Europe entered the war at some stage. There was fighting as far away as Egypt and the West Indies.

The war went badly at the beginning, as Robespierre had said it would. One French general at Lille set out to attack Tournai, just across the frontier in Belgium (you can see it marked on the map), but the Austrian troops forced him back and the same thing happened to a general at Mons.

The Parisians blamed Louis and Marie Antoinette for these defeats. Louis angered them even more when he refused to allow a camp of soldiers from the provinces to remain outside Paris so that the soldiers in Paris could go and fight. This made the Parisians think again that Louis and Marie Antoinette wanted the French to lose the war. The final blow was when Louis dismissed the ministers whom the Parisians liked. The Parisians took it upon themselves to save France.

12 The Fall of Louis and Marie Antoinette

Once more the Parisians came to the rescue of the Revolution. Paris was divided into forty-eight sections. Each formed a guard for the defence of Paris and each also held meetings to discuss the problems of life in Paris and France. The people who came to these meetings were mostly the *sans-culottes*. This really means those who did not wear breeches. This was because they had always worn long trousers, whereas the noblemen and middle classes wore breeches and stockings. You can see this if you look at the portrait of Robespierre. In the picture on the next page you can see what the *sans-culotte* looked like; this man, an actor, is dressed up as a *sans-culotte* for one of the city's celebrations. He is carrying a flag with the colours of France and the words Liberty or Death.

The *sans-culottes* were the workers of Paris who spent their days in the workshops or at dull office jobs or in their little shops and in the evenings they came to the meetings of the section committee to discuss problems. They had always played a great part in the Revolution.

On 20 June 1792 about 8,000 of the Parisian *sans-culottes* broke into the Tuileries armed with pikes to tell Louis how much they hated what he was doing. Louis bravely came out and put on the red cap of liberty and drank the health of the nation, but he knew that the *sans-culottes* were warning him.

The 20th of June was really a dress rehearsal for 10 August. This time the *sans-culottes* had with them the soldiers from the provinces who had just arrived in Paris. These soldiers brought with them a marching song which became the hymn of the Revolution and which is still the national anthem of France—the 'Marseillaise'. You can see the soldiers singing it in the

63

An actor dressed as a Sans-culotte flag-bearer at one of the Revolutionary celebrations

picture on page 68.

The *sans-culottes* were sure that as long as France had Louis and Marie Antoinette on the throne there would be no victory and the Revolution would fail. It was too dangerous to keep them, because the Austrian and Prussian armies had said that they were coming to rescue Louis and the royal family and if anyone tried to harm them Paris would suffer.

On 9 August the *sans-culottes* and the soldiers threw out the town council and put a new one in. The new council was full

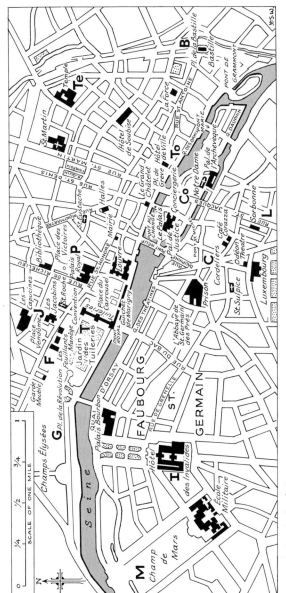

Paris during the Revolution

65

of men who felt as they did. On 10 August the Parisians set out for the Tuileries. The royal family escaped into the gardens and across into the Riding School. Fighting went on between the King's Swiss guards and the Parisians and the Parisians won. In this picture you can see the attack.

The attack on the Tuileries

You can easily imagine how frightened Louis and his family must have been. There were others who were frightened too. These were the wives of the leaders who were organising the *sans-culottes*, the wives of Danton and Desmoulins. You have already come across Desmoulins and will soon read about Danton. This is how Lucille, the wife of Camille Desmoulins, describes the attack of 10 August:

> I had come back from the country on 8 August. Already everyone was very excited. An attempt had been made to kill Robespierre. On the 9th, I had some of the Marseilles soldiers to dinner, and we had quite an amusing time. . . . After dinner we all went to the Dantons'. Danton's wife was crying and could not have been more

unhappy. Danton was in a resolute mood. For my part, I laughed as though I were crazy. They were afraid that the affair might not come off. . . . In the evening we took Danton's mother-in-law home. It was so fine that we took a turn or two in the street. There were plenty of people about. We turned back, and sat down by the café in the Place d'Odéon. A number of *sans-culottes* came by shouting 'Long live the nation!' then some mounted troops; and finally great crowds of people. I was frightened. 'Let's go away', I said to Madam Danton. She laughed at my fears: but when I persisted she became frightened too, and we left. . . . When I got back to Danton's house I found Madame Robert there, and several others. Danton was agitated. I ran to Madame Robert, and said, 'Are they going to sound the *tocsin*?' 'Yes,' she said, 'It is to be tonight.' I heard every word and said nothing. Soon I saw all the men arming themselves. Camille, my dearest Camille, arrived with a gun. O God! I backed into the corner and hid my face in my hands and started crying. But I didn't wish to show such weakness, or to tell Camille before them all that I didn't want him to get mixed up in the business. . . . The *tocsin* rang at the Cordeliers; it went on ringing a long time. All alone, bathed in tears, kneeling at the window, my face hidden in my handkerchief, I listened to the fatal bell. Danton returned. Madame Robert, very worried about her husband . . . ran up to Danton; but he only gave a very vague reply to her questions, and threw himself on his bed. People came several times with news—some good, some bad. [Camille comes back, Danton goes out again and Madame Danton is terribly worried, they go to the Desmoulins' house and then Camille goes away again.]

We had breakfast. Ten o'clock, eleven o'clock passed, without our hearing a word. We picked up some of yesterday's papers, sat on the sofa in the drawing-room and tried to read. Madame Danton read me an article; and it was while she was doing this that I thought I heard the sound of cannon-fire. She listens, hears it, grows pale, and falls down in a faint. . . . We heard shouting and weeping in the street; we thought Paris would soon be running with blood. But we cheered each other up, and set out for Danton's house. People were crying, 'To arms!' We found the door shut. We knocked, called, but no one came to open it. We tried to get in through the baker's shop, but he shut the door in our faces. I was furious. At last they let us in. For a long time we had no news, except that they told us we had won. At one o'clock somebody came to tell us what had happened. Some of the Marseilles soldiers had been killed. But the stories were cruel. . . . Robert had been in the city, and had seen the awful spectacle of the *massacre* of the Swiss Guard. Next day, the 11th, we watched the funeral procession of the Marseilles soldiers. God, what a sight! How it wrung our hearts! Camille and I spent the night at the Roberts' house. I was terrified—I don't know why; it didn't seem that we should be safe at home. Next day on the 12th when we got back, I heard that Danton had been made a minister.

The Parisian *sans-culottes* had won. The royal family were prisoners in the grim tall Temple. There could not be too much rejoicing for the enemy was getting nearer Paris.

The Marseillaise

13 September Massacres

Georges Jacques Danton gave the French courage. In the picture below you can see how strong and tough he looks. He was thirty-three and a great athlete and preferred living in the country to living in Paris. Unlike Robespierre he was very gay and friendly. Like so many of the leaders of the Revolution he was a lawyer. For many months he had fired the members of the Cordeliers Club with love of the Revolution and now he fired the hearts of all the French people to fight and save the Revolution.

Danton

On 16 August the Prussian army had crossed the *frontier*; a week later the great fortress of Longwy had fallen. By the end of August, Verdun the last fortress on the road to Paris, was about to fall too. (You can see these places on the map on page 61.) Danton appealed to the people on 28 August:

There must be 80,000 guns ready in Paris. Those of you who are already armed must fly to the frontiers. How have the nations who have conquered liberty kept it? They have taken it from the enemy, they did not sit back and wait. What would France say if Paris lay *petrified*, waiting for the enemy to come? The French people wish to be free and so they shall be.

Another minister, the Girondin Roland, was also appealing to the French, especially to those people near the frontiers who must have been terrified because the Prussian enemies were getting so near:

Let every town and every *hamlet* man its defences, surround itself with ditches and entrenchments and prepare for a vigorous resistance. Watch the river-crossings and dispose yourselves so as to guard the bridges and highroads. Sow the path of the enemy with obstructions and see to it that he has to *contend* not only with those obstacles but with the *valour* of the people and the army. . . . Nothing must be spared to save the fatherland.

These men were telling the French to be brave and fight back, but the thought of war was very frightening.

In Paris the *sans-culottes* were frightened because they were sure that in the prisons of Paris were men and women, nobles and priests, who were ready to help the enemy. Many were in prison not because they had committed a crime, but because the government, too, was not sure that they could be trusted. People thought that priests and nobles were bound to hate the Revolution and so become its enemies.

The news of the war got worse. Again Danton told the people to be brave and that it did not matter that the enemy was within 140 miles of Paris, that the Prussians and Austrians fighting them numbered about 130,000 men:

The *tocsin* you will hear today is not an alarm, but an alert. It sounds the charge against the enemies of our country. For victory we must dare and dare and dare again; so France will be saved.

70

While Danton was giving strength to the soldiers, Jean Paul Marat was telling the *sans-culottes* in his newspaper called *The Friend of the People*, that they would not get anything good from the Revolution unless they used force. Marat had been a doctor, but when the Revolution came he became a journalist. He hid in attics and cellars because he was always afraid of the government, of the police, of the people whom he had attacked in his newspaper. Like Robespierre, Marat believed that the government must help those who cannot help themselves, it must help those who have nothing, that is, the *sans-culottes*. The government must see to it that the poor had enough to eat and jobs which paid them enough to live on, and there must be schools and doctors and hospitals for them. Every day Marat listened for six hours to the complaints of the poor people who came to see him. In this he was different from Robespierre, who never talked to the *sans-culottes*, and was very anxious for them to be good.

Partly because of Marat, the *sans-culottes* did a terrible thing. They went to the Paris prisons and murdered not only the priests and nobles, but many other prisoners they found there. Why did they do this? One Parisian explains in his diary of 2 September 'Part of Paris is starting tomorrow for the army: the city will have no men left in it: this crowd of unfortunates might have cut our throats while the men were away'. So fear led the *sans-culottes* to murder prisoners for six days. On the next page you can see a grim group of them wearing the red cap of liberty surrounding a poor nobleman.

Many of those murdered in the massacres had done nothing against the Revolution. Some were in prison because they could not pay their bills, some were thieves, some were children in the prison that was used as a *reformatory*. It was so unlikely that any of them had been preparing to cut the throats of the Parisians, that many people were horrified that such a thing had happened.

71

The Abbaye Prison during the September Massacres

14 France Becomes a Republic

On 20 September 1792 a new assembly called the Convention met. As in the other assemblies most of the deputies were lawyers, but this time there were a few *sans-culottes*. The deputies had to give France a new constitution because the 1791 constitution no longer suited France. The deputies also had to help France to win the war.

On 20 September also, the French won their first great victory at the battle of Valmy near Varennes. They drove the Prussian armies back out of France in a fairly easy battle. There was great rejoicing. Danton had been right: if the French were brave enough they would make France free of the

Battle of Valmy

enemy. The Duke of Brunswick leading the enemy soldiers, was sure that the French soldiers who had had hardly any training could not do much damage to his trained and experienced soldiers. However, the French fired back and with cries of 'Long live France! Long live the Nation!' drove back the enemy. This victory changed the course of the war. The French won more victories, so that they even began to conquer lands and bring the Revolution to them. By December the French had conquered Belgium. The French army of the Rhine occupied the town of Mainz. Everywhere they went they brought the Declaration of the Rights of Man and liberty, equality and fraternity.

In the Convention there was not very much fraternity. There were now roughly two groups. One group was usually called the Girondins; the other group was called the Jacobins, because the leading speakers were members of the Jacobin Club, or the Mountain because they sat together in the higher part of the hall. The two groups soon began to quarrel. However, the first thing they did pleased everyone.

The Convention declared that France was no longer a monarchy, that is, a country in which the head of the government is a king whom the people can never choose; it was now to be a republic, where the people do choose their leader. In 1792 a republic was very unusual, although today you can probably think of quite a few.

This was the final break with the old France. The French even were to change their dress-fashions to show that France was different. In the picture opposite you can see the result. The couple on the left are saying 'Oh! how old-fashioned and out-of-date!' to the couple on the right who are saying 'Oh! how foolish the new look is!' You can see that the fashionable man had a hairstyle which was much more like that of the *sans-culottes* for he wore his hair long and did not bother to have a powdered wig.

74

Fashions old and new

The Convention now became the centre of quarrels. The Girondins felt that Paris and the town council and the *sans-culottes* were getting too much power. The Girondin leaders, for example Roland and Vergniaud, were a little jealous of Danton and Robespierre and Marat, the leading Jacobins, because the people liked them and listened to them. On the whole the Girondins were more interested in the wealthy, the land-owners and factory owners, while the Jacobins preferred the poor.

The great problem they had to settle was what should they do with Louis, no longer king of France, and now known as Louis Capet.

Some of the deputies wanted Louis to have a trial so that he could defend himself; others thought no trial was needed. Some thought that because Louis had tried to help the enemies of the Revolution he must die. The Girondins did not want Louis to die; Robespierre and the Jacobins felt that he must die.

Louis had a trial. He knew perfectly well that he did not

have a chance. In the picture below you see Louis at the right of the picture with a book in his hand. He is saying:

In speaking to you for the last time perhaps, I declare that I am innocent of the crimes you accuse me of and have nothing to reproach myself with.

The Trial of Louis XVI

However it was no good. The keys held up below him were keys which opened a box in the Tuileries in which were found papers which proved that the royal family wanted to get help against the Revolution.

The deputies found Louis guilty. They now had to decide whether or not Louis should die. The voting went on for a whole day from the evening of 16 January to the evening of 17 January 1793. Each deputy had to get up and go to the raised platform and say whether he thought the king should go into *exile*, or go to prison, or die. No clear decision was reached on that day, but on 19 January more deputies voted for death than voted for exile or imprisonment.

On Tuesday 21 January, Louis left the prison of the Temple in a closed carriage and armed soldiers took him to the Place de la Révolution, the former Place Louis XV. Citizens carried guns and pikes to prevent anyone from trying to rescue him. The sound of drums drowned all shouts and screams. To the men who were holding back his arms so that he should not try to run away, Louis said, 'I hope that my blood may assure the happiness of the French people.' Louis then spoke his last words to the people: 'My people, I die an innocent man.' The crowd heard no more as the drums began again. Then, as you can see in the picture, the executioner held up Louis's head.

The Execution of Louis XVI

The people shouted, 'Long live the nation! The tyrant is dead.' The Revolution had destroyed all the powers of the king and now it had destroyed the King himself, because to the people this weak and gentle man was a tyrant.

15 War and the Girondins

After Louis was dead the deputies still had other troubles to deal with. The war continued. The Girondins said 'We cannot rest until all Europe is ablaze.' They and Danton wanted the war to spread throughout Europe, to England, to Germany, to Italy, to Spain, to Holland, so that the Revolution would spread too. All nations would one day be free; as in France, the unjust privileges would go. The nobles and clergy would lose all, but the poor would gain wealth and happiness. The slogan of the war would be 'Loot the castle and spare the cottage.'

On 1 February, France declared war on George III and England. England then had the greatest power over trade and the sea and so the war was going to include great sea battles. On 11 February, the French general Dumouriez invaded Holland. In Belgium, which was still in French hands, the Revolution was spreading.

The war went badly for France. Two things therefore happened. Robespierre and Danton said that there must be a committee, a small group of leaders who would save France. This committee became the Committee of Public Safety about which you shall hear more. The second great event was the attack on the Girondins.

The Parisians were sure that the war was going badly because the Girondin leaders were not being careful enough. They were also sure that some of the Girondins were not loyal to France and were helping the enemy. When General Dumouriez, the general whom the Girondins had chosen, went over to the enemy and deserted France, the Parisians made up their minds that the Girondins must go.

The Girondins had attacked Marat, the Parisians' hero. The Girondins preferred the rich to the *sans-culottes*. They did not want to make laws to fix prices of food which would help the *sans-culottes* to buy bread. They did nothing to punish the men who kept stores of grain to themselves while others around them starved for lack of bread.

Parisians came home to hear that their brothers had died in battle, parents heard that they would never see their sons again, children heard that they would never see their fathers again because of the terrible war. All this was not the fault of the Girondins, but the Girondins got the blame all the same.

On 31 May the officer in charge of the National Guard in Paris took over Paris and posted soldiers at all the gates leading out of the city. The soldiers arrested some of the Girondin leaders. On 2 June soldiers marched to the Convention which still met in the Tuileries. The *sans-culottes* came too. This time, unlike 10 August, no one was killed, not one soldier fired a gun, but the Parisians got what they wanted. The Girondins fell from power.

Paris had saved the day. The Commune, the town council of Paris, reminded everyone in France that Paris always came to the rescue:

> The Parisians were the first to start the Revolution when they overthrew the Bastille, because the Bastille lay most heavily over them; and so again they have overthrown the new *tyranny* because they were the first to see it.

The fall of the Girondins meant that their rivals the Jacobins came into power.

Although in Paris many people were now pleased with what had happened, in the French provinces there were many peasants, for example, who were angry and felt that the Revolution was not bringing them a better way of life. They disliked having to leave their fields and go into the army.

To please these discontented peasants, the Convention did what it could not have done when the Girondins were there. It brought in laws which gave the poor peasants more land. The deputies also brought in a new constitution, the Constitution

79

of 1793. Robespierre did a lot of work for this and put into it many of his ideas. The Constitution said that the laws of the country existed to make the French people well and happy. Some of the things it said were very new, although today we have all the things Robespierre wanted to bring. It said that everyone should have the chance to have a job, to go to school and learn, to have enough to eat, to be able to get help when one is ill or old or cannot get a job. Everyone was pleased about this Constitution but because there was so much trouble in France, lots of these ideas did not become laws and so people were disappointed. Discontent and trouble were spreading throughout France.

16 Enemies at Home and Abroad

Near the west coast of France lies the area of the Vendée which you can see on the map on page 21. Here thousands of peasants were ready to follow noblemen and clergy to fight against the Revolution. They were religious people and disliked what the Revolution had done to the Roman Catholic Church. They also liked to have a monarchy rather than a republic and wanted the son of Louis XVI to be king.

In the south of France, in the Gironde, at Marseilles, Toulouse, Bordeaux and at the great silk manufacturing town of Lyons, there were many who disliked the Revolution for different reasons. They were businessmen; many of them were wealthy and they were afraid that the Jacobins, under the influence of the *sans-culottes* of Paris and leaders like Jean Paul Marat would attack them and their wealth. They were ready to fight. In 1793 these men organised an army. They wanted to march on Paris and destroy the government. In July, this army of rebels was getting near the river Durance; once across it, the path to Paris would be easy. The government sent soldiers to fight back, but one of the only ways of preventing the rebels' advance was to cut the ropes which would help them to cross the Durance. Joseph Agricole Viala offered to do this; the soldiers said no; he was too young for he was only thirteen. Joseph would not take no for an answer. With a gun in one hand and an axe in the other he went to the river. He first fired at the enemy who were dangerously near, then throwing down the gun, he cut the ropes with the axe. The rebels saw what he had done and fired at him and killed him. He became a great hero of the Revolution and was buried with other great men in the Panthéon in Paris.

Another discontented part was in Normandy, in the north of France. In July a beautiful young woman named Charlotte

Corday left Caen in Normandy and came to Paris. On 13 July she went to buy a knife in the shops in the Palais Royal and then went to see Dr Marat who was away from the Convention because of illness. She found him writing at a desk over a bath in which he was sitting. She talked to him about the rebels in Normandy and then got out the knife and stabbed him to death. To her Marat was a monster who would only do evil to France, so she murdered the friend of the people. In Paris the people heard the news with horror and great sadness. The painter David, who was a friend of Marat, painted the picture you see below in memory of his friend.

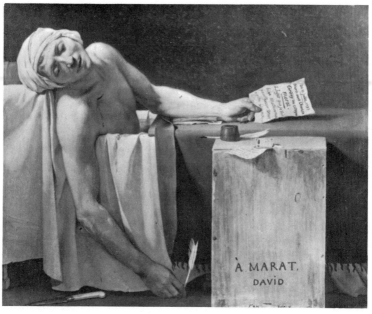

Death of Marat

Charlotte Corday, sure that she had done the right thing, wrote to her father a few days before she went to the guillotine: 'Forgive me, my dear papa, for having taken my life into my own hands without your permission. I have avenged many innocent victims'.

The murder of Marat shows the division of France, that the French were ready to kill one another, but France had to be united to attack the enemies abroad. England, Holland, Spain and Prussia and Austria were all trying to get into France. English ships were stopping French ports and ships from trading and prevented food from getting into France. The French had to fight back.

On 23 August there was a call to every French citizen, man, woman and child to come and either fight or help in some way:

> From this moment on until the enemies have been driven out of the territory of the Republic all French people are permanently enlisted for the service of the armies. Young men will go and fight; married men will forge arms and transport supplies; the women will make tents, and clothes and will serve in the hospitals; children will make old linen into bandages: old men will be carried to the squares to put courage into the fighters and to teach hatred of kings and to teach republican unity.

This appeal was to everyone in France, because the Revolution had said that all are equal so all must fight in every way possible. For hundreds of years people felt that wars were the business of kings and ministers, but now this war was the concern of everyone. The wish to beat the foreign enemies was the thing which really kept the people of France together.

It was up to the rulers of France to get rid of the enemies inside France and outside France. The most important of the rulers were the twelve men of the Committee of Public Safety.

The Committee of Public Safety met in a room which had walls lined with green wallpaper and sat at a table covered with a green cloth. They met at eight o'clock in the morning every day and worked until ten at night or later. The most important members were Robespierre and Carnot who organized the army; the young Saint-Just and the crippled Couthon, but all of the twelve played a part in getting rid of the enemies of France.

83

17 Darkness over France

On 5 September 1793, the people of France learned that their whole Mediterranean fleet was in the hands of the British at Toulon. This was terrible news as it meant that they were almost without help at sea.

In Paris the people were so angry that Toulon had let this happen that they marched on the Convention to demand justice. Suddenly a great darkness came over France and the whole of Northern Europe at twelve noon. The marchers could not move, they were so surprised and frightened. There was an eclipse of the sun. On this day the Reign of Terror began.

A member of the Paris town council got up and said:

It is time for all Frenchmen to enjoy that sacred equality that the Constitution assures them; it is time to bring in this equality. Make terror the order of the day.

You remember the Great Fear at the beginning of the Revolution? Well, terror is a great fear, but the difference now was that this time the new rulers of France deliberately made this fear. The rulers, in order to bring equality and freedom, also brought fear and terror. It was a ghastly thing to want to do, yet the Parisians wanted it. The committees of the rulers, especially the Committee of Public Safety, wanted it and saw to it that terror did come to France. They believed that the Constitution of 1793 could not be followed because France was too weak and divided. So Saint-Just got up and said that the government of France must be revolutionary until the peace, that is, that the government could bring in the terror and that the Committee of Public Safety could have all the power it needed to do so. The Terror was like the eclipse of the sun.

The months between September 1793 and July 1794 are usually known as the Reign of Terror.

Why did terror reign? Terror reigned to defeat the enemies

Saint-Just

of the Revolution at home and abroad.

Terror reigned to organize the army and keep it supplied with food and guns, so that it could drive away the Prussians, the Austrians, the Spaniards and the English who were trying to defeat France.

Terror reigned to make France one strong country, instead of a country in which one province fought against another province.

Who brought the terror? Mainly the members of the Committee of Public Safety. They could not do all the work by themselves and so they got help from members of the Convention, who became special representatives, sent to the armies and towns, to the eastern frontier and the towns fighting against the Revolution. You can see the splendid uniforms they wore in this picture.

A Representative of the Convention sent to the armies and towns

More help came from the grim Revolutionary *Tribunal*, and the committees all over France who watched the people. If someone felt that his neighbour or fellow-worker was not loyal to the Revolution, he could report him to one of these committees. In the picture below you can see what it was like in one of these revolutionary committees. You can see the anger in the men's faces.

A meeting of a Revolutionary Committee

The Revolutionary Tribunal was in Paris and the chief judge was the hard-working Fouquier-Tinville. Those men and women whom he sent to die usually went in carts to the Place de la Révolution to be guillotined. The guillotine was the invention of Dr Guillotin and it was supposed to kill quickly and without pain.

The Revolution, the Republic, the Nation, these were what mattered. They were more important than the 17,000 French men and women whom the Revolutionary Tribunal and committees sent to their deaths and the 500,000 people the various committees and courts throughout France sent to prison. They were more important than the few thousand people who died because of the terrible prison conditions and the ten or twelve thousand who died without a trial during the wars of the Vendée, who were shot or drowned in hundreds.

Robespierre, who once upon a time had refused a job because it might involve ordering the death of men and women, now wanted the death of all those whom he felt were dangerous to keep alive. He himself would give up everything for the Revolution, even his life, so others could also do this. The young Saint-Just agreed with him.

18 Enemies of the Revolution

Robespierre and the Jacobins and the *sans-culottes* felt that the rich were wicked and they were always ready to attack them so that they could help the poor. They introduced a law which others before them had suggested. It stopped the price of food from getting too high. They had to do this for the Parisians sometimes got so angry that they went into shops and altered the prices of food themselves. The Jacobins brought in laws which said that anyone caught hiding food in his house would go to the guillotine. They forced the rich to lend money for the army.

France also had to get ready to face the enemies abroad. Three members of the Committee of Public Safety set out to make a strong army and navy. The Tuileries gardens became shops and factories where men came to make guns. Every church bell had to come down and be melted down for gun metal. Food had to come from every possible place for the use of the armies. An army of 50,000 men, poorly dressed, some of them riding on starved horses because there was still not enough food to feed both man and horse, following officers who had little more experience than the men they led, went into battle. They cheered themselves up by singing the Marseillaise and they attacked the enemy at Wattignies (you can see this on the map on page 61), and they won a great victory on 16 October.

On the same day in Paris, the woman whom so many felt was still the greatest enemy of the Revolution went from a cell in the Conciergerie to her death after a terrible trial at the Revolutionary Tribunal. The woman was Marie Antoinette. Fouquier-Tinville asked her questions, but whatever answer she gave she knew it was useless. The courtroom was full of those who wanted her death. Robespierre hated the cruelty of the trial but still he wanted her to die.

Marie Antoinette on the way to the guillotine

In this picture you can see how much she had changed since the portrait you can see on page 4. She was on her way to the guillotine when David drew this portrait. She went to her execution like any ordinary criminal. She died amidst the shouts of 'Long Live the Republic! Long live the Nation! Down with Tyranny!'

Two weeks later, on 31 October, the Girondin leaders, those who had lost power in June, also went to the guillotine.

With the great ones going, what was life like for the ordinary person? Life was very different during the Terror. There was even a new calendar, with no Christmas Day; and it was not 1793 but the 'second year of liberty'. You had to carry with you a card on which was your name and address. You had to have a ration card for buying food. You were not able to earn more than a certain amount. You could say nothing against the Revolution. You got used to seeing carts taking victims to the guillotine, a few of them were your friends. There were even some women who sat in the Place de la Révolution and watched and counted the heads as they fell while they knitted.

The Jacobins did not want to be cruel: they wanted to bring peace to France but they were still sure that the only way to do this was to go on hunting out the enemies of the Revolution and killing them when they found them.

19 Terror in the Provinces

Lyons was the second most important city in France, It produced silk and was as important in France as Manchester in England. The people of Lyons were fighting against the rule of Paris; they were the wealthy fighting against the poor and against the Revolution. As long as Lyons fought, France did not have a chance of getting the English out of Toulon.

The Committee of Public Safety therefore persuaded the Convention to declare that:

> The city of Lyons shall be destroyed. Every habitation of the rich shall be demolished: there shall remain only the homes of the poor . . . the buildings employed in industry and the monuments devoted to humanity and public instruction.

The Committee then sent Couthon and Collot d'Herbois to Lyons. They arrived on 4 November and almost the first thing they did was to order a guillotine. Collot d'Herbois said, 'We must sacrifice feelings for a person to feelings for the people.' In other words it does not matter if a few die if the nation is saved. On 25 November the troops arrived and their commander described the scene:

> Terror was painted on every face. The deep silence that I took care to recommend to our brave troops made their march even more *menacing* and terrible. Most of the shops were closed. A few women stood along our way. In their faces could be read more indignation than fear.

Ten thousand women petitioned for mercy for the thousands in prison. Collot d'Herbois and his men told them that it was nothing to do with them and they should go back to their kitchens where they belonged. By April 1794 the members of the Committee of Public Safety and the representatives of the Convention from Paris had put to death two thousand people in Lyons. This was to be an example to the rest of France, to show what would happen if any other town dared

Massacre at Lyons

to attack the power of Paris and the Revolution. Men were lined up and shot and many were killed as you see in this picture. Fortunately the government did not succeed in destroying Lyons.

In the Vendée the people were still fighting for the return of a king and the nobles and the clergy. They, of course, were the worst enemies in France. The Committee of Public Safety therefore sent men to deal with the enemies. Soon the prisons were so full that Carrier, the man in charge, ordered whole boatloads of prisoners to be drowned in the river.

This is why those months of 1793 and 1794 deserve the name of the reign of terror.

No part of France escaped some form of terror. Saint-Just went to Alsace to help the army, but this meant interfering with people's lives and getting money and clothes from the rich and the poor to give to the army. In Brittany, Saint-André saw to it that the ships were ready to attack the English.

He also organized the lives of the people of Brittany. They had to go to political meetings, they had to go to the theatre to see patriotic plays, so they could not even choose what they did with their spare time. There were spies everywhere ready to report people who spoke against the Revolution, so everyone had to watch his words.

This was the ghastliness of the terror. It is so difficult to understand it, because the terror brought back the cruelty, the tyranny and the hard life that the Revolution had wanted to wipe out.

20 Robespierre

Robespierre was in power in Paris, and in the rest of France. He was not alone. He ruled with the Committee of Public Safety and they must all share the praise or blame, but Robespierre was stronger than any of the other members. He wanted the French to love the Revolution as much as he did, and to be as unselfish as he was. He still wanted to help the poor and the sick, but once he thought he saw an enemy of the Revolution, then he was without kindness. He was not like the other leaders of the Revolution. He is difficult to understand because, in a way, he lived in a world full of words, instead of living, as most of us do, in a world full of people. To him the Revolution came before everything and this is why he let his friends Danton and Desmoulins die.

He had already sent to the guillotine Hébert and his supporters because he felt that they were harming the Revolution. Hébert had wanted the Terror to become even more cruel, especially towards those people who still wanted to go to church and have the religious processions they had always had.

To be as cruel as Hébert was wrong in Robespierre's eyes, but to be as gentle as Desmoulins and Danton wanted was also wrong.

Danton and Desmoulins wanted the Terror to end. The rebellion in the Vendée was almost over. Napoleon Bonaparte, a young Corsican soldier, had saved Toulon which was now in French hands again. Camille Desmoulins was writing articles in his newspaper which attacked the reign of Terror. He wrote:

> I shall die in the opinion that to make France republican, happy and flourishing, a little ink would have sufficed and only one guillotine.

In other words he thought that the thousands of deaths were unnecessary. Robespierre did not agree and he was sure that for Desmoulins and Danton to feel this was dangerous for they both had influence on many people. He and Saint-Just collected information which made the court find both of them guilty and on 5 April 1794, they went to the guillotine.

Hébert, Danton, Desmoulins had gone. Who was left to lead the people? Only Robespierre and the Committee of Public Safety. Robespierre was the man the people of Paris had cheered because they knew he could do no evil. Yet he lost their love by trying to make them as good as he thought he was.

Robespierre wanted people to be perfect. He wanted them to prefer good deeds to money. He wanted them to have a new religion, the religion of reason. He organised great processions in which he took the leading part. There were great days of celebration with pageants designed by David, the painter of the picture of the Tennis Court Oath and the Death of Marat. These pageants were quite magnificent. You can see one of them in this picture:

Festival of the Supreme Being

Cardboard figures which represented evil beliefs were burned in great fires. Good citizens helped to plant trees which were called trees of liberty. Robespierre was always the leader at these festivals. He stood high above the crowds of Parisians in the Champ de Mars and made speeches in which he praised freedom and good sense which he called reason. In spite of these marvellous pageants, was this the religion the French people wanted? The answer is probably no. Instead of church weddings there were dull weddings without the beautiful music. There were no church bells any more and none of the festivals they were used to and liked. Robespierre, however, took no notice of their wishes because he thought this new religion was best for them.

Robespierre wanted to make the French people good, and to do this he had to take away those people who were evil, or else they would make more people evil. On 10 June a new law came in which meant that those whom the police took to the Revolutionary Tribunal were very likely to go straight from there to the guillotine, for prisoners were hardly given a chance to defend themselves in a trial. The guillotine killed twice as many people in Paris in June as in May and three times as many in July.

Why must the Terror go on? The guillotine was now killing, not the noblemen and the priests, but shopkeepers, office workers, grocers, servants and peasants. The war was going well; on 26 June there was a magnificent victory at Fleurus (see the map on page 61). The Terror had come so that France would be prepared for victory over the enemy and now this victory was coming, the Terror no longer seemed necessary.

In Paris people began to think that the Terror was going on because Robespierre wanted it to. The other members of the Committee of Public Safety were afraid that he would send them to the guillotine too. The *sans-culottes* were angry because Robespierre and the Jacobins had fixed wages at a certain

Battle of Fleurus

amount so they could not hope to earn more money. Robespierre's plans for more money and help for them were not coming to anything.

July got hotter and hotter, more and more carts of prisoners went to the guillotine, more and more people were afraid.

On 27 July, Robespierre and Saint-Just went to the Convention. They both knew that there was danger. Robespierre made a long speech. He reminded the deputies that the French Revolution was the first revolution in the history of mankind which was based on the rights of man. It was too wonderful an event to be ruined by selfish people who put their interests first, before those of France, and those of the Revolution. These selfish men must go. Robespierre was expecting the impossible. None of the deputies in the Convention, none of his fellow-members of the Committee of Public Safety felt safe in Robespierre's presence and so they now arrested him, together with his brother Augustin, Saint-Just, the crippled Couthon and his friend Le Bas. The Convention felt that these men were tyrants, and the Revolution could not allow tyrants to live.

The prisoners managed to get to the Town Hall, where their supporters were gathered. There was still hope, they thought. Surely the *sans-culottes* would remember that they were their friends who had always tried to help them, surely the *sans-culottes* would rescue them and punish the Convention? The *sans-culottes* did nothing! At two o'clock on the morning of the 28th, soldiers arrived at the Town Hall. Saint-Just went quietly. Le Bas had two guns: one he used to blow out his brains, the other Robespierre used to shoot himself in the jaw and so the soldiers carried him on a stretcher and took him away from the Town Hall. They brought him to the room next door to the green meeting-room of the Committee of Public Safety.

Soldiers coming to take the wounded Robespierre to the Conciergerie Prison

You can see the wounded Robespierre in this picture. Then the soldiers came and carried him to a cell in the Conciergerie. Afterwards he went before the Revolutionary Tribunal. There was no trial; everyone knew he was guilty. At six o'clock in the evening of the 28th, Robespierre went to the guillotine.

The man whom the Parisians had once cheered and called the Incorruptible was dead! He had died amidst the shouts of 'Down with the Tyrant'.

'The most important rights of man are freedom and self-preservation'. This is what Robespierre believed. The *sans-culottes* believed it too and let Robespierre die just because they thought that he was taking away their freedom. Robespierre died, but the things he believed in did not die. Freedom, equality and the brotherhood of man were what everyone wanted. The rulers who came after him in the summer of 1794 tried to wipe out everything that the Jacobins and Robespierre had done. They failed. No one had as much power as Robespierre had had until Napoleon Bonaparte came to power. Napoleon did not try to forget what Robespierre had done. Many of the things Robespierre had wanted for France, Napoleon brought. He brought the schools; he saw to it that when citizens came before judges, the judges treated them all equally. This is what the French Revolution had wanted—equality, liberty and fraternity. The French people never forgot this and never forgot that they had the right to attack their rulers if they allowed themselves to forget this.

CONCLUSION

You have read of many deaths and much cruelty, but this was only part of the story of the French Revolution. The French did not want this cruelty; it was the price they had to pay in order to get liberty, equality and fraternity. Many revolutions have taken place since 1789; you can probably think of some. Today in Africa and in America there are people who are fighting for liberty, equality and fraternity. They are saying what the French said, that if anyone attacks these rights, then they have the right to fight back. They say what the Declaration of Rights says, that we are born with equal rights.

100

HOW DO WE LEARN ABOUT THE FRENCH REVOLUTION?

From London you can get to Paris by boat and train in about twelve hours, and a day or two in Paris is the best way of learning more about the Revolution.

The Paris you see today is not the same as the Paris of 1789 because in the nineteenth century Napoleon III and his minister Haussmann made many changes. Fortunately they did leave lots of places which the Parisians of 1789 would still recognise.

Not far from the streets with the lovely shops, the Rue de la Paix and the Rue de Rivoli, is the Rue St Honoré. At No. 398 stood the house where Robespierre lived. He could easily walk from here to the Place de Marché St Honoré where stood the Jacobin Club. It was also not too far to walk to the Tuileries and the Convention. The palace and the Riding School have gone, but you can walk in the Tuileries gardens and, if you get tired, can sit on the marble benches, beyond the round pond where children sail their boats. The Convention put up these benches for the old men to sit on while they watched the athletics matches and perhaps urged the young men to go and fight for the Revolution.

From the Tuileries you turn west and come to one of the most beautiful squares in the world, the Place de la Concorde. The name means the square of agreement and peace, but during the Revolution, it was called the Place de la Révolution (square of the Revolution). By the fountain nearest the river stood the guillotine which killed Louis XVI, Marie Antoinette, and so many others during the Terror.

Nearby are the gardens of the Palais Royal, where Camille Desmoulins made his famous speech, and where all the Parisians used to come for their Sunday and evening walks and discuss the news of the day. In one of the shops Charlotte Corday bought the knife with which she murdered Marat.

The Bastille has gone, of course, but you can see where it was if you go to the Place de la Bastille and look for the white stones. North of it is the beautiful Place des Vosges which must have looked very much like this during the Revolution. Not far away stood the Temple where the royal family were prisoners.

In the Ile de la Cité, the oldest part of Paris, is the Palace of Justice. Here you can see where the Revolutionary Tribunal met. You can visit the Conciergerie where Marie Antoinette was prisoner.

In the Latin Quarter off the Boulevard St Germain is the Cour du Commerce, at No. 8, Marat's newspaper was printed and at

No. 9, Dr Guillotin worked. In the Rue de l'Ecole de Médicine the Cordeliers Club met. In the Panthéon you can see where Rousseau is buried and where for a time Mirabeau and Marat were also buried. Nearby in the Rue St Jacques is the Lycée Louis-le-Grand where Robespierre and Camille Desmoulins went to school, but this is not the building they knew.

Near the Invalides, where the Parisians came in search of guns before they attacked the Bastille, is the famous Eiffel Tower and beyond is the Champ de Mars where so many of the celebrations of the Revolution took place.

There are many more places to see in Paris which will help you to see what Paris was like during the Revolution. Just to be in Paris and watch and listen to drivers arguing in a traffic jam and friends discussing politics at a café table helps you to imagine how the Parisians of the Revolution must have talked and argued.

By train you can reach Versailles in about half an hour. Here before you get to the wonderful palace, you can visit the Tennis Court, the scene of the famous oath.

When you see the palace, you can imagine what it must have been like when it was the home of one of the strongest kings in Europe, and you can see what the Revolution has done to it—made it into a museum. Inside you can see Louis XIV's bedchamber with the balcony on which the royal family appeared to the crowds of women on 5 October, 1789.

If you walk across the magnificent gardens you will come to the Petit Trianon, the favourite house of Marie Antoinette. You can see that it would take a long time for anyone to disturb her here. The dining room has a painting of the ballet in which Marie Antoinette and her brothers, including the Emperor Leopold, danced at Schönbrunn. In the gardens you can see the farm and the dairy where she liked to be.

If you cannot go to Paris then try to get pictures of these places. If you can go to Hampton Court, you can see a royal tennis court which is quite like the one in Versailles. A library will probably have a copy of Arthur Young's *Travels in France*, which will give you some idea of France before and during the Revolution.

WHERE DOES ALL THE INFORMATION COME FROM?

Just as today in England there are special reporters who take down the speeches our ministers and members of parliament make, so during the Revolution there were reporters who took down the speeches made in the National Assembly, and so we can read these too. Many people kept diaries, for example the Englishman Arthur Young and the American Gouverneur Morris. Many French people wrote the story of what happened to them during the Revolution. Necker's daughter, Madame de Staël, wrote a book about the Revolution. There are many letters of Mirabeau, and Robespierre and Marie Antoinette. There are the newspapers which Marat and Camille Desmoulins wrote. There are the cartoons like the ones you saw on page 23 and page 49.

If you are in Paris and have time to go to the Carnavalet Museum, you can see lots of things which tell the story of the Revolution. There is a clock with the Revolutionary calendar. There are fans with pictures of the events of the Revolution. There are paintings and drawings, some of the many pictures of the Revolution you have seen in this book. In museums and even in antique shops in France you can sometimes see plates with scenes of the Revolution painted on them.

THINGS TO DO

1. Describe a day in the life of a nobleman at the court of Versailles before the Revolution began.

2. Why do you think the Revolution happened? Have a class discussion about this.

3. Write a short play about the fall of the Bastille. You can have lots of people in it. You can begin with the scene in the Palais Royal when Camille Desmoulins made his famous speech.

4. Was Robespierre a good or a bad man? Have a class debate about this.

5. Pretend that you are a TV interviewer and that you have to go and interview Parisians after the execution of Louis XVI, and then have to go and interview people in the Vendée. Write down your questions and the replies the people gave you.

6. Do you think that the story of the French Revolution would make an exciting film? Which events would you put into it?

7. Make a wall chart of the main events of the Revolution with pictures to illustrate them.

8. During the Revolution lots of mugs and bowls had pictures or slogans of the Revolution on them, for example 'Long Live Liberty!' If you do pottery, make a mug or a bowl and decorate it like this. Or make a paper fan and decorate that.

9. Describe the life in Lyons during the Terror.

10. If you could take part in a revolution what would you like this revolution to change?

GLOSSARY

This is a list of special words. If the word you want to know is not here, look for it in your dictionary.

abdication, giving up the throne

abuse, something done in the wrong way

administrator, man who helps to bring the government's laws to the people

assembly, a group of people meeting together

cardinal, in the Roman Catholic Church the cardinals are the priests who are the princes of the Church. Only the Pope has more power

compensation, something given to make up for losing something else

constitution, the rules which say how a country is governed

contend to, to fight

courtiers, the nobles who live at the king's palace

dapper, neat and smart

declaration, announcement

deputy, someone who speaks or does a job on behalf of others. In France the deputy is like our M.P.

despotism, unlimited power which is not always used in a good way; a ruler who uses power in this way is a *despot.*

émigrés, people who leave their country, usually because of a revolution to live in another country

equality, having the same as everyone else

estate, class of people

Estates General, the *assembly* of the *deputies* of the three *estates*

exile, being away from one's own country, not at one's own request, but because it is dangerous to remain in one's homeland

finances, managing money

fraternity, feeling of brotherhood and that all people belong to one another

frontier, imaginary line showing where a country ends

grievances, things to complain about

guillotine, a machine for beheading people.

hamlet, a small village

harangue, a very dramatic and exaggerated speech

hardiness, a mixture of boldness and strength

incorruptible, cannot be made to do a bad thing

intolerable, something you cannot put up with

journalist, a person who writes for a newspaper

legislative, making laws

liberty, being able to do what one wants to do; being free

livre, a French coin worth about 5p of our money

105

majority, the greatest number

massacre, the murder of lots of people at the same time

menacing, threatening and frightening

merchant, trader who buys and sells goods usually to and from foreign countries

orator, a man who makes great speeches

parlement, group of judges meeting in an *assembly*

petition, a request

petrified, unable to move because of fear

political society, country which has a government and laws

posting-master, the man in charge of the post

privilege, a favour or a good thing that some people have and others do not

reformatory, house where children who have committed a crime have to stay

renounce to, to give up

sentiment, feeling

tocsin, alarm signal

tribunal, court which decides what to do with people accused of having committed a crime

tyrant, a ruler with the most power in the country which he uses to be cruel; the rule by a tyrant is called *tyranny*.

valet, a man servant who usually looks after the master of the house

valour, brave deeds